The Public Image

of the corporation executive is still that of the totally enveloped "organization man." Walter Guzzardi's brilliant and surprising book shows that this stereotype is passé. The young executive of to-day is a new breed: pragmatic, strong-minded, and superbly efficient. He is challenged by a job that will bring him responsibility, authority, the opportunity to exercise his potentials to the limit; and he seeks out the company that offers him these. He is brilliant, but non-intellectual, a man of vast tech-married, has a college degree, 2.8 children. He tends to be Republican.

A major expansion and recast of his celebrated *Fortune* series, *Walter Guzzardi's* incisive profile of the young executives stems from more than one hundred lengthy and confidential interviews with industry's rising executives, backed up by several thousand questionnaires sent to major corporations. *The Young Executives*, which includes an Introduction by Peter F. Drucker, is destined to become the successor to William H. Whyte Jr.'s *The Organization Man*. It is an invaluable guide to the unwritten rules of corporate conduct as practiced by the men on their way to the top in the powerful world of industry.

"In some ways *The Young Executives* is to the business world what the Kinsey Report was to the psychologists. It is a candid look at the ambitions of the young men in the grey flannel suits."
—*Distribution Age*

Other *MENTOR EXECUTIVE LIBRARY* Books

MODERN MARKETING STRATEGY, *edited by*
Edward C. Bursk and John F. Chapman
The most up-to-date methods involved in transferring goods
from producer to consumer. Selected from the *Harvard Business Review*. (#MQ623—95¢)

NEW DECISION-MAKING TOOLS FOR MANAGERS,
edited by Edward C. Bursk and John F. Chapman
How mathematical programming can most effectively be
used to solve business problems. Taken from articles in the
Harvard Business Review. (#MQ624—95¢)

THE CONCEPT OF THE CORPORATION
by Peter F. Drucker
An up-dated edition of the classic study of General Motors
—the company that has become the model for modern large-
scale corporations across the world. (#MT569—75¢)

THE MANAGERS *by Roy Lewis and Rosemary Stewart*
An examination of the English, German, and American executive, comparing and contrasting them on the economic
and sociological levels. (#MT342—75¢)

The Young
Executives

How and Why
Successful Managers Get Ahead

WALTER GUZZARDI JR.

Introduction by
Peter F. Drucker

A MENTOR EXECUTIVE
LIBRARY BOOK

MENTOR

Dedication:

For A.B.W.

Third Printing

Mentor Trademark Reg. U.S. Pat. Off. and Foreign Countries
Registered Trademark—Marca Registrada
Hecho en Chicago, U.S.A.

MENTOR EXECUTIVE LIBRARY BOOKS are published *in the
United States* by
The New American Library, Inc.,
1301 Avenue of the Americas, New York, New York 10019,
in Canada by The New American Library of Canada Limited,
295 King Street East, Toronto 2, Ontario,
in the United Kingdom by The New English Library Limited,
Barnard's Inn, Holborn, London, E.C. 1, England

First Printing, July, 1966

PRINTED IN THE UNITED STATES OF AMERICA

Contents

Introduction

Men of the generation of World War I—the Johnsons, Er-hards, de Gaulles, and Maos—still hold the top positions in all major countries and in most of the important areas, whether government, science, trade unions, or business. But the young-est of them are rapidly approaching sixty. And the reins are therefore fast falling into the hands of the next generation, the generation of World War II, now forty-five or under. What manner of men are these new leaders, the "Young Execu-tives"? This is the question Mr. Guzzardi raises and answers in this fascinating book.

Of course individuals in this generation vary as much from one another as they have varied in every generation since the beginning of Man. But still a generation has in common cer-tain experiences it has had and certain experiences which, though very important for its predecessors, it has not had. And the new and specific experiences of the men who are now in their forties, the Young Executives of Mr. Guzzardi's title, were indeed distinct and different. Their introduction to adult-hood was World War II with its tremendous demonstration of the power of large-scale organization, its planning, its empha-sis on technology, and its worldwide scope. By contrast the war of 1914, which so deeply molded the world view of the older generation, was still fought largely on the same Euro-pean battlefields on which the Roman legions had bled and died, and by infantrymen who were closer in their training and equipment to Caesar's legionnaires than to the missile age.

The new generation of Young Executives also is the first generation in human history to take for granted universal higher education. Nine out of ten of Mr. Guzzardi's Young Executives are college graduates. One third have gone to grad-uate school.

Finally this is the first generation that takes for granted the existence of large, indeed very large, organizations. It started its adult life in the largest of them all—the modern military service. It went from there to a large and rapidly growing university. And it is making its career and its living in the big business corporation. It lives and works, as a rule, in the modern metropolitan area, whether New York, Chicago, Boston, or Dallas. By contrast the men of the preceding generation, the men now rapidly approaching the twilight of their lives and careers, grew to manhood when large organization was still seen as the exception rather than the rule. Even though no longer born or reared in the "log cabin" the politicians of President Johnson's generation still typically came from the small town or the farm as Mr. Johnson did himself. The politicians of the next generation—typified for instance by the Kennedys —are products of the big city. And the same shift in what is considered the typical environment has occurred in respect to business executives, labor leaders, educators, and so on—outside of the United States as well as here.

Mr. Guzzardi confines himself, of course, to the study of one group, the successful young executives in business. This is perhaps not quite as much of a limitation, however, as it might seem. For in the years in which these men started their working lives, in the Forties and early Fifties, the ablest and most ambitious of our young men tended to be attracted to jobs in big business. One reason was undoubtedly that this was where the opportunities then were: American business was on the whole overage at the end of World War II if only because there had been so few opportunities for advancement during the long depression of the Thirties. Another reason was probably that the big companies, during this period, started for the first time to recruit able men aggressively on the campus—and no one else did this for quite some time. Finally this generation had been delayed by the war and therefore felt it needed to make good money fast; and big business was, between 1945 and 1965, the one employer offering good money to a beginner.

The Young Executives in business would not, I imagine, be as good a sample for the next generation, the generation that is now entering upon adult life. Indeed that today other careers, notably teaching and government service, appear as attractive to the young, able men as business, may be one of the very big changes and one of the very big differences between the generation Mr. Guzzardi reports on in this book and the next generation, which will take over ten or fifteen years hence. But for the generation now emerging at the top the young business executive is probably fairly representative.

What then characterizes this group?

"They live to be effective," Mr. Guzzardi reports. "Effective" may be the key word altogether. They get things done. They are task oriented. They want results—and are willing to work hard to get them.

"They are highly professional in their approach to their job." "What are the facts?" is their first question. They are much more concerned with "what is right" than with "who is right." They believe in doing things systematically; they plan, they think things through, they measure. And accomplishment means a good deal more to them than the money.

On the whole they are a very decent lot—remarkably free of prejudices, of resentments, of envy. But as Mr. Guzzardi points out they also lack a good deal. To call them "superficial" would be doing them an injustice. "Unimaginative" might be more fitting a term. They are active in church and community. They are good husbands and fathers. They read a good deal. But they do these things because it is expected of them rather than because they care deeply or have thought and felt deeply. As Mr. Guzzardi points out, they admirably manage a symphony orchestra in their town but may neither care much for music nor know anything about it. For all their fine qualities they are, to put it succinctly, somewhat philistine. They do not differ in this respect from the great mass of men and of mankind's leaders throughout the ages. Still it is not too difficult to see the attraction that the "beatnik"—the eccentric for eccentricity's sake—has for the next generation now growing to manhood.

Finally Mr. Guzzardi's Young Executives lack the very quality most people outside of, and unfamiliar with, the big business organization would have expected to predominate. There is not one "organization man" in the lot. No one works for a computer—though a good many have computers working for them. There is, the Lord be praised, very little mealy-mouthed cant about "this great company," very little "company loyalty" in these self-portraits. No one sees the need to "conform," let alone the urge to do so. Practically all of the men see the very essence of their job in making their own top management change itself and the company. An amazingly large number attribute their success to their opposition to higher authority or to their defiance of company tradition. And they do not *have* to conform. They know that they are in demand and can leave and go elsewhere; indeed most of them have done just that at some point in their careers.

Indeed, reading this book, I could not help feeling that the myth of the "organization man" and of the "corporate octopus" reflects nothing more than the fears of the older generation before the new, and therefore frightening, phenomenon of large-scale organization that arose during their lifetime. The Young Executives treat it with the contempt bred by familiarity. After all, their first adult experience came in manipulating the largest organization of them all—the United States wartime military establishment. And not one of them is worried over what big business will do *to* him. They all ask, "What can this big business do *for* me?" To them the large organization offers freedom of action, opportunities for achievement, and room for effective self-expression. To them, in other words, the organization is what it should be—a tool of the individual.

This book rests on a more solid foundation of research and study than a great many pretentious sociological treatises. But it is a reporter's book—in its fast pace, its readability, its reliability, and its timeliness. It is a reporter's book also in that Mr. Guzzardi leaves implied his own concluding question rather than spell it out. It is an important question, however. For this book asks in effect: How can the next generation of leaders, the generation now growing into manhood, add to the solid foundation of competence, effectiveness, and professionalism what today's Young Executives lack: wisdom, values, and commitment? The Young Executives, as Mr. Guzzardi describes them, represent a very big step forward from the "old executives" whom they are so fast replacing—above all in their effectiveness. But they are concerned mainly with means, and indeed admirably accomplished in using means. They have not, Mr. Guzzardi brings out clearly, bothered their capable heads too much about ends—and this job the next generation will have to tackle.

Peter F. Drucker

Montclair, N. J.
Summer 1965

Preface

Since man first eyed woman speculatively across a fire at the mouth of a cave, the thought of organization has been irresistibly attractive. Its magnetic appeal, however, obviously goes beyond the primal urges. Almost as basic as those urges is man's desire to examine the organization—to analyze how he came into it, what he gives to it and gets from it, why he continues to put up with it, and how much significance it has in his life. Like other men, writers have often found themselves harassed, confused, compelled, and driven by some form of organization to which, voluntarily or not, they belonged; but they have never been so harassed or confused or driven that they have been unable to find the time or the means to set down their thoughts and their responses to organizational manifestation which they may have accepted, or against which they may have rebelled. While the proof of the point would lie beyond the reach of any concordance, organization has probably been as much written about as motherhood—and in some cases for the same reasons, since the two subjects are not unrelated.

The study of organization raises a thousand complicated questions. They range from matters of high importance concerning man and his liberty—the validity of the justice meted out in wartime or in other times of high national passion, for example, for what were the issues in the Dreyfus affair, or the Sacco-Vanzetti case, if not ultimately questions of the organization against the individual?—to such fascinating anthropological minutiae as the effect of social organization on the children of Dakota Indians, who are taught that it is impolite to give replies to questions unless everyone who is present knows the answer. Included in that spectrum of issues—not, to be sure, at the ultraviolet or infrared terminals, but in a significant middle band—is the matter of the individual in the business organization, and the questions of freedom, ethics, and conformist behavior that membership in so peculiar an institution raises. Aristotle, an early observer of management, perceived that "the art of getting wealth is the business of the manager," and in the twenty-three centuries since he made that remark—one can assume it was not a platitude then—commentators have been embroidering on the theme.

To that long and complicated history, this book is intended to be a short and modest footnote. The book is eclectic, since it borrows freely (although with appropriate credit lines) from the thoughts of many of the people—some authors, some merely witnesses—who have expressed themselves in the field. But it is also original, not from any special gift of the author but because it draws upon and acquires much of its argumentation from primary source material.

That material took two forms. A large number of young executives, perhaps in the end about a hundred, consented to lengthy and intense interviews, of varying degrees of formality. During the course of these talks, they were surprisingly frank and outspoken about themselves and their business lives. Perhaps the most compelling parts of this book are those italicized portions where the young executives are permitted—at long last, one can almost hear them sigh with the restless impatience that is shared by so many of them—to speak for themselves. Their own speech, and the generalizations and interpretations that their own speech led to, came forth in the end as the most important source for this book.

Second, under the auspices of *Fortune*, several thousand questionnaires were sent out to young executives, by means which are explained in Chapter 10. The replies to that far-ranging questionnaire, whose line of inquiry followed the personal inclinations of the author rather than any set sociological form, lend credence to the book's general argumentation.

The young executives were specially selected in accordance with special criteria. To put it briefly at this point—the matter is explained fully in the text—they are young men on the train, convinced that they are going somewhere, and knowing that the conviction is shared by their superiors. There is no implication in this book that the young executives are archetypes of businessmen everywhere. The young executives are an extant breed of manager, but how many of them there are in the business world at large, how long they will be the way they are now, how they will turn out in the end seems to be anybody's guess. It would be a fascinating exercise to interview them all over again ten years from now. By then, they may be at least as different as they are, at this moment, from the organization man of the 1950's.

It has become a commonplace, in a preface, for the author to recall the moment when the idea for his book first struck him. He awoke from a daydream at high noon, perhaps; or he was hit by a shaft of light at some dim and smoky hour. Nothing would be more satisfactory than to be able to recount here such an instant of visitation. For the journalist, however, fact must take precedence over inclination. This book began as an article in *Fortune*, and that article, in turn, began in the office of Duncan Norton-Taylor, *Fortune*'s managing editor. Norton-Taylor sent the author out on an assignment to report on and then to write about young executives, since Norton-Taylor suspected, through some osmotic process known only to managing editors, that something worth saying would turn up. Thus the original idea was his, although, in the best tradition of *Fortune*, the writer was left to develop that idea in his own way, and come to his own conclusions. The firmest conclusion of all, of course, is the one that Norton-Taylor saw so clearly at the beginning: there was, indeed, something to say. There was enough for four articles in *Fortune*. There was enough for this book, which expands and revises those four articles, and adds a good deal of new material to them. The author is indebted to Norton-Taylor for his original insight, and for the generous time he allowed for the author's thoughts and views about the young executives to jell and take form in print.

A further prefatory commonplace would include a long list of people without whose help neither articles nor book would have been possible. Once more, fact must take precedence over tradition. There is no one, with the conspicuous exception of the young executives themselves, whose assistance was vital to the reportorial and writing process. But there are several people, besides Norton-Taylor, whose kindness and competence helped to improve this product in significant degree. Max Ways, who was *Fortune*'s editor most closely associated with the series of stories, made many useful and stimulating comments about the organization, the language, and the content of the stories as they progressed, and those comments had a great deal to do with the success of the *Fortune* series. A man whose views are sometimes alarmingly original and disturbingly well supported, Max Ways also displayed—and the author knows how difficult this must have been for him—considerable forbearance when he came to portions of the manuscript with which he could not agree. Miss Patricia Hough, a research associate on *Fortune*'s editorial staff, assisted the author in research and in checking the manuscript. *Fortune*'s Mary Grace did the proofreading with rare attention and precision. *Fortune*'s Brooke Alexander was a helpful and amicable colleague throughout.

For all of that assistance with the development of interpretation and with the accuracy of facts, however, the author remains the book's main agent. The views are essentially his, and throughout the book—especially in those extensive parts of the argument that appear here for the first time—his must be the sole responsibility. Where there is disagreement over a point, dissent from a thesis, wrath over a commentary, let them fall upon his head. No one need share them.

Chapter ONE

The Man and the Myth

His wife and children smile out at him from a silvered frame. On the walls may hang a reproduction of a Remington Indian, arrested forever in his headlong gallop to give the alarm; tacked alongside of that suspended drama may be an indifferent copy of a Corot landscape. Diplomas bearing his name and embellished with the appropriate ribbons and seals, add their touch of professionalism. A carpet of no memorable pattern or color covers his office floor. Through the window whose light falls across his desk different panoramas may be visible: the long, low buildings that make up a manufacturing complex in New Jersey, or the churn of traffic in a downtown Pittsburgh street, or the fronds of a palm waving above a reflecting pool in Florida, or merely the similar windows of similar buildings in Manhattan whose prospect reflects his own. Whatever the geography, the atmosphere within is much the same: it is busy, and probably noisy, with none of the hushed aura that surrounds a boardroom or the office of a chief executive. Behind his desk, comfortable in that atmosphere, sits the man himself. He is clean-shaved and respectably neat in a suit bought off the rack and altered, where absolutely necessary, to fit. The need for decent integument thus fulfilled, the man has turned his attention to the matters at hand. He is the young executive. He is facing today's problems.

Much depends on the solutions he finds. He and men like him, taken together, constitute American industry's most critically important resource. They give the element of life to every corporation; without such men, as one analyst has written, "the resources of production remain resources, and never become production." Taken together they make up the one ineluctable advantage that one company can have over another. Even so recently as ten years ago, this self-evident truth was not so apparent to many big companies. But now, the giant corporations—Standard Oil of New Jersey, General Electric, General Motors, and many others—have become acutely aware that their whole future may turn on the imagination, the judgment, and the competence of their young executives. These managers have become a social class—and one can really call them that—of pivotal importance: a fact of remarkable note by itself, but even more surprising in view of the rapidity with which the class has emerged.

The corporations that employ these men, of course, have other sources of strength. Plants, machinery, patents, products, capital assets, all form part of a big corporation's arsenal, and from them often come the means by which companies can score tactical gains in the short run. But such advantages are likely to be canceled out, after a brief period, by a leap-frogging competitor with a newer patent or a new product. In the long pull, the securest advantage a company can have is the advantage of having and keeping able people in responsible positions. Whether companies falter or prosper will depend in the end upon the abilities of their young executives—the abilities of the men who, so properly suited, now come before our eyes.

What breed of men they are, how they came to enter the corporate environment, where they react sympathetically to it, when they collide with it, what authority they have within it, how they find freedom in their sharded world—these are the topics for examination in this book.

The young executives are men who meet two criteria, imposed by definition at the outset of this study. The first is the criterion of age: they are men who range in age from the early thirties to the middle forties. They are not trainees. They are the solid performers who are polished by ten, fifteen, or even twenty years of business experience, most of it in the employ of big companies. There, for the most part, they still work. Despite their lengthy experience, they are in corporate terminology still "young."

The second criterion is one of position in the world of business. These men are not the young geniuses or the whiz kids burst fresh from the egg who are tracking a jet trail through the business sky. The thirty-year-old president of a big company who shot up like a cork is not among them. Also omitted is the forty-five-year-old manager who has ceased to move up, is losing his interest in moving up, and stolidly awaits retirement. The young executives are men who occupy positions on the upper slopes of a big corporation. They are not yet at the pinnacle, but in rank they have already left the ruck of their contemporaries behind. They have moved rapidly through several tiers of the corporate hierarchy, and they are now located on that key ground whose precise boundaries elude definition, but whose general location is nonetheless clear enough. The ground abuts the areas occupied by top management. The young executives, after their decade or more of progress, now find themselves in some way proximate to the top officers of their company: they may report to the top regularly, at least regularly enough to be recognized—they may be seen, for example, conducting occasional briefing sessions around the oval table in the paneled boardroom of Standard Oil of New Jersey. Or, they may be charged with responsibility for working on projects or running departments in which their company's top management takes a continuous interest: they may run an electronics division for G.E., for example, or a consumer products division for R.C.A. In short, they stand where they can see both the substance that top management deals with, and the shadow that it casts.

Thus, by the standards of the business community he dwells in, the young executive has already achieved a good deal. And he has more to look forward to. In the jargon of the personnel directors, he is called "promotable"—a clumsy enough word, but one with the magic to summon up some pregnant visions of the future, some expectations that seem heady and powerful to this ambitious man. In those expectations, the young executive is more than likely going to prove correct. More responsibility and authority, in the corporate scheme of things, surely lie ahead of him. His superiors in the organization are very conscious of the fact that he is coming on strong. They are reluctant formally to name him duke or prince, and he is just as reluctant to wear such a crown, not from any sense of modesty but because of his own accurate estimate that its weight may slow him down by causing him some embarrassment in the eyes of his colleagues, or because its display may stir up resistance to his ideas from his peers or subordinates. Nevertheless, although crown remains invisible and title still tacit, many of these men are very much in the corporate line of succession. Over the next ten to fifteen years, new chief executives for many a big company will be chosen from among the ranks of this generation of young executives.

There stands the young executive—in his early prime, in a promising business position. He and the men like him came to that promontory from many diverse climates and soils. The young executive comes off the paved streets of the Bronx, where he may have gone to a poor boy's public school; he comes off the oilfields of Oklahoma, where some of his schooling, at least, came from watching his father climb oil rigs; he comes from the open farm country of Ohio or Pennsylvania, where life on the farm soon came to look to him like a life long on work and short on rewards. He may have been taught strict morality in the lap of a close-knit southern Baptist family, and he may carry those rigid standards with him today. Or, alone in a big-city rooming house, he may have written out his own morality play before he even came of age. His father may have been a banker, who left him some money; or a businessman, who left him some business interests; or a failure, who left him to his own devices. One man's father is a butcher—"happy and, by his own standards, successful." The father of another is a guitar player. One man's mother has a doctorate in economics; the mother of another never made it through grade school. Dissimilarities between these men are ubiquitous and manifest. Only the matrix, America, is the same.

The men now inhabit many different business worlds. The young executive may be supervising an accounting department, making it expert in the new instruments of the trade. He may be directing the design of hotel rooms or the design of space vehicles. He may be plotting an orbit around the earth, or plotting the movements of crude oil in the international market, or simply plotting a new move against a competitor. Or he may have charge of the sale of phonograph records or razor blades or ladies' shoes or faltering companies. He may be buying steel, or buying wisdom. The young executives sprang from all the rich variety of America, and they are dispersed now through all the rich variety of American life.

But at the core of their diversity lies homogeneity. These men have a communality of intellectual characteristics. They share important and distinguishing attitudes, aptitudes, and abilities, which, just as much as their age and their corporate position, serve to make them as identifiable as if they wore a jewel on their collective forehead. But in spite of the fatuous adjurations of the ordinary management book ("Look for the clear-eyed, flat-bellied man," confided a recent one. "A relatively young man with a roll of suet around his middle probably won't stand up to the requirements of long hours and split-second thinking. . . . Moreover, he will very likely prefer the easier course of action, regardless of performance criteria"), these men do not wear such badges of distinction. They do not have common physical traits visible to the eye or susceptible to discovery by tape measure. The young executives are bound together by many ties, and, whether the men are piggybacking freight out of Chicago or buying rosewood for a hotel chain in Boston, the ties assert themselves. But all the significant ones are ties of the mind.

The young executive is serious, with the abiding seriousness about his business that is a precondition to all business success. He is aggressive, confident, independent, and decisive —aggressive in his views toward competitors within his company or outside of it; confident in his ability to survive, to outrun, to win in the end; independent in his business views, to which, with proper allowances at certain times, he may cling even if he is a minority of one; and decisive in his approach to any problem, an approach which typically does not merely intend to learn and to analyze, but which looks at the problem as an opportunity, as a chance for action and accomplishment. All those qualities seem to have been a part of his natural character and mental structure since he began to mature; and often that process of maturation seems to have begun early, showing itself with a determination of purpose and a single-mindedness that became apparent at school age.

His mind is a tool machined for business. It is inquiring and acquisitive, and the young executive has trained and polished it until it has become an extraordinarily effective instrument with which to attack the entwined problems of his business life. He has a peculiarly objective way of regarding his experience and his mental capacities, almost as though they were like a bank account or a stock holding: they have a present and future value, they can fluctuate depending on the market, they are to be employed in the most advantageous financial way. No matter how good his personal financial condition, he regards his own mind and its storehouse of business lore as his greatest asset; from that disinterested estimate stem many of his other attitudes and proclivities.

His greatest pleasure comes in the relentless use of that mental machinery. Work, the application of his trained intelligence, occupies his life. He works hard partly because of the competitive fires that burn within him, partly because he forever seeks "more challenge and more responsibility"—his favorite words for explaining his own appetites—and he believes that hard work can attain for him those twin desiderata. That engrained inclination vigorously to apply his mind toward definite goals gives him his strong propensity toward pragmatism: he strives always to effect changes in the external world, changes that he can then hold out at arm's length and admire. But he can admire them only briefly, until the urge to make another change, or another improvement, comes over him. The period of admiration may last an hour, or a day. It is not likely to leave him suffused with pleasure for longer than a weekend.

Academically he is a narrow man. He burns up his intellectual energies on the job, making his beloved external changes. He has few interests outside of his business that engage his intellectual curiosity. In the eyes of the academy, which sometimes looks askance at such pragmatists, the young executive is scarcely an intellectual at all; the academy's view needs some correcting, but it also contains some truth, for this young and successful businessman is not cultured, if being cultured means having an educated sense of the history of man, a curiosity about where the learning of the Western world came from, and where it may lead. He is bereft of such a sphere of sapience. His kind of narrowness, his sort of incompleteness, at present may be a somewhat fugitive quality about the young executive; but, like other fugitives, it is likely to return to trouble him some day. When business involves him, as it may, in the larger social questions and the grander social designs, he may find himself confused and handicapped—a condition that seems to him now to be inconceivable, but that may come about nonetheless.

But now, in his chosen country, the young executive's interests are broad enough. He either is or is in process of becoming what the business community calls "a generalist"—a man who may have some technical background, or some specialized strength in marketing or manufacturing or sales, but who has considerable familiarity with and interest in other areas of business too. He uses his totally engaged intelligence to perceive relationships between the various fields of business which may be subtle and tenuous. Those relationships, the interstices between specialties, are likely to attract the young executive's curiosity as much as the more familiar and defined provinces of managerial activity.

Toward his company—toward that entity which has been capitalized in thought and writing as The Organization—the young executive maintains a complex cluster of attitudes. He grew up in the corporate milieu, he lives there, and he accepts that milieu as natural for him. The big corporation is to his mind an essential feature of the modern business landscape. To him it seems natural, therefore, that at some times and in some ways harmony should characterize his relationships with his company. Obviously, he does not want to lead a revolution against the corporate life, or against the company that he works for. To become that kind of a revolutionary would involve asking passionate questions, and finding passionate answers to broad and basic issues. This young businessman, with his bent of mind, will never raise such issues. He regards them as settled long ago.

While he is no revolutionary in that sense, he is yet in a very important way, in his business context, a rebel. His greatest psychic gratification, his ego satisfaction, comes when he succeeds in making a change of an important kind in his company's or his industry's business methodology. The process of making such a change he calls "creating something"—and "creating something" is a central aim in his life. To gain the satisfaction that such "creation" brings, he will dissent long and loudly from the organization's established methods. He will raise his voice in committee and in meetings with his superiors. If the issue is important enough, if the dissent runs deep enough, if he concludes that the weight of company bureaucracy will keep his creation from coming into being, he will leave the organization for another—with only the briefest glance back over his shoulder. He will pause, for a moment perhaps, with just a twinge of regret over cutting the strands of friendship with some associates; but the associations that go beyond the surface camaraderie that daily contact requires are not very numerous, and reconciliation to their loss is not very hard. "I like the people I work with in this company," says one young executive. But he makes clear that the sentiment will not anchor him to the organization: "I like lots of people I meet outside the company, too," he adds quickly.

Thus the principal importance of the organization to the young executive is the opportunity it offers him to gratify his own drives. Through the organization he can develop his private self, and for that reason more than any other he stays with it, and works within its walls. He does not love the organization. He does not want to be loved by it. He believes it is better for both of them if they do not love each other. He does not seek security through conformity with the organization. His security lies within himself.

But from currently popular portraits, one could scarcely recognize the man at all. His image has been drawn variously, and with flourishes, but its general cast has rarely been favorable. In some renditions, he has been looked on not as a man but a mole, tunneling his way through corporate life. In others he is nothing so innocent as a mole, but a schemer selling himself for profit—a kind of latter-day Faust who has turned in his cape for a gray flannel suit and a button-down collar. In still another version, he pursues only materialism, and in the pursuit he becomes not Faust but Peer Gynt, running, and losing sight of his goal, and finally losing himself.

Whatever the vesture attributed to the man, the central point made about him is that he leads a life of sham. He is said never to show his genuine, but only his cosmetic, self; indeed, in the end, he may be discovered not to have an inner, genuine self at all. He is called an alienated man—not alienated from society by choice, as the artist may be (there is more validity to that kind of alienation) but alienated because he dived deep into the organizational currents of our time, and disappeared; alienated, one might almost say, by immolation. In the last century Oswald Spengler passed the typically funereal judgment that "all things organic are dying in the grip of organization . . . the individual is now entirely without significance," and, as one would suspect, the alienating villain now is still the organization—a disembodied power that somehow bowdlerizes men.

These simplistic views, which purport to describe a whole man, have been applied to the young corporate man with an especially crude and heavy brush. In these versions, the young executive is not demoralized, since he lacks, indeed has always lacked, the preconditions of awareness and sensitivity that are implied by such a state. Instead, without even being conscious of it, he has given up his individuality, handed over his power of choice, and surrendered without a fight—to the only enemy in sight, the corporate environment. Group Think is the only ratiocinative process left to him. To dissent from the judgment of the group would be abhorrent. To make a decision on his own responsibility would be traumatic. In some of these renderings, the corporate executive sports the badges of indistinction: egg-walking past the tough problems, suppressing the tiny whisper of his true views, honoring compromise above all things. He hates to bet—but if he must, so runs the fiction, he bets neither on the red nor on the black but on the gray, because he is gray himself, just a particle in a gray immensity.

Peace and security are his desiderata; the boss is his household god. One writer in this vein described a business type as "only a mass man, incapable of choice, incapable of spontaneous, self-directed activities . . . a creature governed by his own conditioned reflexes. . . . The handsomest encomium for such creatures is 'They do not make trouble.' Their highest virtue is 'They do not stick their necks out.' " Once this creature was a free man; but now his environment—the big company he works for—has clamped him in chains, and so pitiful is his condition that he counts the links among his friends.

This concept that the organization is somehow taking a grip on a man and making him into an automaton—taking a man who would have been a strong advocate of truth intelligently arrived at, and changing him into a faceless blur—has long roots. Part of the concept is compounded from the myths of the past.

The dead hand of the past presses most heavily in the assumption of a dichotomy between man and his environment—a popularly accepted but, on analysis, an impossible and an unreal dichotomy. That assumption appeared in social theories over two centuries ago—theories which held that man was born free; that he once lived in an idyllic state of nature; that he forswore those happy conditions when he made a social contract, and agreed to live in the midst of other men. By so doing he fell to this side of Paradise, and found himself among evils he was never made to face. All man's ills—so recounted seventeenth-century philosophers like John Locke, and eighteenth-century philosophers like Jean-Jacques Rousseau—spring from his dealings with other men. Man, surrounded by men, can never again know the kind of happiness he enjoyed when he lived in those lonely but blissful caves. Among men, only the hermit is free.

Modern philosophy and social science have long since confuted those views of the old social philosophers. Anthropology and biology have exploded the myth of man's former unfettered existence, beginning with the evident biological facts that man is born not free but tied to his mother, and that he remains for years more dependent on the surrounding social structure than any animal. Emerson wrote that "all men have their root in the existing social system." John Dewey added that "we cannot regard environment as a deus ex machina."

Psychologist Erich Fromm stated that "there is only one productive solution to the relationship of individualized man to the world—his active solidarity with all men." In a passage emphasizing man's social nature, John Gardner, President of the Carnegie Foundation, and now Secretary of Health, Education and Welfare, in a book called *Self Renewal* gave the coup de grace to "romantic notions of complete individual authority" by pointing out that "a loss of the sense of community . . . [could bring] all the accompanying disorders of self regard." We now know that in the distant past the free regions were roamed by very few men, and most of the others were like most Greeks in the age of Pericles—just slaves in the Laurium mines.

Who understands and accepts this truer relationship between man and his environment does not love freedom less than the myth-makers. There was no more redoubtable champion of liberty in modern times than Judge Learned Hand, but he commented in his *Spirit of Liberty* that "man is tied to all men, as all men are tied to him, in a web whose threads no eye can follow and no fingers unravel." As for the dangers of belonging to a committee, Hand said: "The larger part of my official life I have been in a court where three sit together, and that seems to me of immense advantage. The joint judgment of three is worth more than three times the judgment of one, unless he is a genius." Intelligent love of and effective defense of freedom can come only after man is put thus properly in his social context. Only then can modern social perils be met. It is imperative to understand that of us all, the hermit wears the heaviest chains.

But many observers of the modern business world have not been listening. At the heart of their protest—and much of the extant writing about the business world is an expression of protest—they postulate the happy age invented by the anti-social philosophers of the eighteenth century. They refer to a blissful state of nature that never was. They ignore the realities of the historical past. They have largely overlooked, as David Riesman has written, "the terror, misery, and disorder of the status society of the past which they so much admire, while underestimating the tremendous achievements of modern men in making themselves comfortable in the face of the novelty of a fluid industrial society. . . . Americans of the more mobile classes have not only adapted themselves to a fluid society, but they have also begun to adapt the society to their own needs . . . liberating people and their movements from the chain-mail of etiquette. We are well aware of the vices of the money-grubber, and perhaps less sensitive to the meanness of spirit that develops in a monastery or in a university, where wealth as a goal is minimized."

Surely this corrected view has been amply aired. Reviewing a book called *Alienation: The Cultural Climate of Our Time,* in *The New York Times,* Harold Rosenberg commented that "for the majority of mankind, any basic incompatibility between a Self and a Social Mask (or Non-Self) is unreal—at most, genuine opposition appears only temporary. . . . It is typical of the alienation philosophers to contrast the fragmented twentieth-century city-dweller with the whole man of some earlier paradise of togetherness—the Florence of Michelangelo, a South Sea island (before the white devil docked, of course), a Southern plantation with a chorus of darkies in the background." Rosenberg concludes: "It is difficult to be convinced that there is less selfhood in 1964 than there was in 1464 or in 64."

The organization man, popularized a decade ago by William H. Whyte, Jr., was one of these non-self creatures. Organization men, Whyte wrote, "are the ones of our middle class who have left home, physically as well as spiritually, to take the vows of organization life. . . . Between themselves and the organization they see an ultimate harmony and, more than most elders recognize, they are building an ideology that will vouchsafe this trust. The urge is to unity . . . just as the group has obscured the role of the individual in creation and discovery in research and communication, so in the regular work of running an organization it is obscuring the function of leadership. Anti-authoritarianism is becoming anti-leadership. The young man can become a true believer in the organization. Of all people in organization life, he is best able to reconcile his own modest aspirations with the demands of the organization. The average young man cherishes the idea that the relationship with the organization is to be for keeps."

This Whyte man, when Whyte first described him ten years ago, was occupying the lower middle and middle ranks of a big company. He was twenty-five to thirty years old then. Whyte found him to be "a man at rest, at peace with his environment, and broadened by suburban life . . . obtrusive in no particular, excessive in no zeal." Now, a decade later, the most competent of those organization men have become the young executives. Not unpredictably, they have turned out far better than their critical elders thought possible. They have become obtrusive in many particulars and in many zeals.

And their relationship with their organization is emphatically not for keeps. Rightly, Whyte remarked that "every organization needs at least one son-of-a-bitch to keep it alive and alert to its obligations in a changing world." Ten years later, we can make one important amendment to that statement—it takes a lot more than just one. If by a "son-of-a-bitch" we mean a prickly, fact-armed man who is quick to dissent, who can be persistent and often downright annoying in his disagreement, and who, if he starts to lose for reasons he thinks unfair, will pick up his marbles and move to another game somewhere else—then there are plenty of sons-of-bitches among the young executives in the big companies today.

The failure of many writers about the business world to give proper weight to that view has resulted in other failures. They have failed also to catch up in their portraits the true essence of corporate man himself. They have misunderstood his motivations. They have misread the nature of the modern business organization, largely because they have not perceived the new shape that the organization has had to take on in order to survive in its world of sweeping change. And they have misjudged the special kinship that obtains the most able of young businessmen and the organizations that they work for.

Listen to Them Talk

One young executive, now forty-four, has been working for more than twenty years for his New York company, in its long-established cement division. His early interest moved him into marketing, and there he has elected to stay. How much does harmony with the organization mean to him?

"I believe in what I'm doing. This company needs to expand its product-development organization—orienting the product to the consumer. We've got to promote harder—promote cement against aluminum and steel. We've got to make more calls on architects, construction engineers, maintenance engi-

neers, traffic engineers, showing them what we can offer, getting into their design plans early. If a building using steel is
being planned, I want to be able to say more than just 'Struc-
tural concrete is good, too.' I want to say, 'Give me your functional designs. Give me some lab time. I'll show you that concrete can do what you want aesthetically—at less cost, or with
a better job.' That's the marketing concept. Some time ago I
found that none of our young salesmen knew one man in the
traffic section in the state highway department—they made all
their calls on purchasing. But the traffic man is the one who
designs in asphalt or concrete. I want to arrange it so that we
call on him with a man who knows traffic engineering.

"Our line salespeople don't agree. They would just as soon
have all of us marketing men take a slow boat to China. For
years they had a product, and the customer was there, and all
they had to do was sell at a price. These sales managers—they
always look at me with a fishy eye.

"In a company this size, you can write something out and
put on a grandiose demonstration before a high-level audience.
But when you're selling a business philosophy, you start at the
bottom, and prove your point as you go along. That way, marketing has made a lot of progress around this company. Some
people say I'm the one who built it up. But I'm a problem
child. In marketing, we couldn't have done all we've done by
having people in this company say no to us and then accepting
it. We've gone around them. I never made any personal enemies, but I have a lot of business enemies who stand in my
way and say that it can't be done.

"Some of that may sound bitter. I'm not bitter. I just want
to change some things around here. In a couple of years they
ought to create a top spot in the company for marketing. By
that time I will have been here twenty-five years. I'll have a
good income. But I won't let them say to me, 'Now, good old
Jack, be patient.' I'll be ready to reply: 'I've given this thing
my lifetime and if a top job isn't in the offing, you owe it to me
to tell me and I'll get out of here.' I could stay on and get fat
and satisfied. People tell me that I'd be a fool to quit after
twenty-five years. But I'd die inside. Who wants to do that?
This situation should be settled soon. I'm ready. And my wife
knows all about it—as far as she's concerned, I could quit
tomorrow and do whatever I had to do."

That man is aiming at a fundamental change in the corporate structure and the established habits of a great company.

He has already been successful to some degree in securing what he wants. But in a manner characteristic of his generation, he is not yet satisfied. He never will be.

Another young executive, at thirty-eight, is a branch manager in the Midwest for a big electronics company. He heads a staff of engineers and salesmen for electronic data-processing equipment. His office remitted about $20 million to New York headquarters last year. How much does he suppress his true views about the organization?

"I spend a great deal of time battling the octopus—all the emanations of this big organization. The district manager, the regional manager, the staff men—I'm always on the phone squawking to them about something. I'm always pounding the desk in conversations with my bosses. If I think the competition may beat us out because we can't get delivery for the customer on time, I'll fight to get the equipment out of the normal rotational order. Of course, I say we'll lose the order for sure if we don't get the equipment—that's what my salesmen say to me. But headquarters is getting pretty hardened to that argument by now. They hear it from everybody and it becomes more or less routine. So I say that if we lose the order we may lose some related opportunities; the customer may give us a black eye in the whole area. If I think something serious may go down the pipe, I'll really howl to New York, Chicago, everywhere.

"My salesmen are all on base salary plus commission. I am myself—we have an annual quota and if we make it, it could mean a $10,000 bonus to me personally. If we make double the quota, my bonus is doubled. The company fixes the quotas in some weird way. Nobody understands it, but it isn't very scientific. I really scream when I get the quota, telling them how impossible it is and how unfair. Then I work like hell to make it.

"That quota means all kinds of pressure on me. But if we lower our prices after we hear about a competitor's bid, we're in trouble. I've got to move carefully. Yet I want the business and, within limits, I know they want me to get it. I go pretty far sometimes. I even make some commitments in writing about what we're going to be able to do. I'm taking a hell of a risk—if a customer ever passed on a letter like that to New York I'd be out on the street, no question about it. I go around all day with my neck out a mile. But I wouldn't change it.

"When we opened this office, the company's top executive vice-president came out for the opening. We have this very nice, innocent little arrangement for him, and then he turns to me at the meeting and asks, 'Well, what are the problems?' Right away I'm in a tough spot. If I say there are no problems, he wonders what he needs management for. If I say there are some, he'll pass it on to someone else in the organization and it might lead anywhere. I had a couple of problems, and I told him about them, and the situation got pretty tense. But I think I did the right thing, even though nothing changed anyway. It's an example of how working for a big company increases the risks instead of diminishing them.

"But having this big company behind me means a lot. We're not the biggest, but we are very big, and we can do so much more than just about anybody else. I don't know how I'd feel if the apple started shrinking. We talk pretty cynically around here about what we're doing, and about the customers and the competition. We sound pretty hard-boiled, and in the heat of the fight I guess we are; there isn't much we wouldn't do to get an order. But we stay within the decent bounds of doing business, and deep down we get some secret satisfaction about what we can do for people. Lots of companies around us, in the largest industry in this area, have been hard hit lately. One of them, though, showed a profit in the last half for the first time in four years. I'm convinced that we helped to keep it alive. Nobody knows how long it will live. But it wouldn't have survived this long without us.

"Sometimes I think I'd like to run my own business. I guess it would be easier. But then I get kicks out of running this place, and I run it like it was my own, and it's worth $20 million a year. And my future is tied up with this area just as though this were my own business. If industry here really began to die, it would mean I just couldn't meet my quota. Sure, the home office would understand what had happened—but the response would still be, 'Why couldn't you get some more business?' Nobody wants to hear about why things didn't go well. On the other hand, let's say industry here took a jump ahead. I'd get my share of that jump, revenues would go up, and I'd be a hero. Everybody would be slapping me on the back. There's nothing that this company likes better than a guy who's lucky."

That man has made dissent into a way of life. He does not want to tear down the organization's walls—he accepts the organization, even though it is multilayered, resistant, and inflexible—but he does want to rearrange its furniture to suit him better. His primary objective is to overcome the resistance that the organization offers to his individual action. Against what John Dewey called "the pressures of institutional rigidities," he pits the strength of his own individuality and the authority of his own knowledge. The personal responsibility that he carries is no lighter than the ones carried by the romanticized figures from the romantic age of rugged individualism—it is simply a different kind of burden.

Chapter TWO

The Man and His Attitudes

The traits and the attitudes that distinguish the young executives are quite different from the ones that the myth-makers have attributed to them. But common traits most certainly are shared by these men, and from them one can put together a kind of composite man—a prototype of the successful young manager in big business today.

The first of the common traits to surface was the early desire that most young executives felt to acquire a thorough education. In high school or college, the young man who was later to become a member of this executive generation discovered the value of education as a tool, and he soon set about fitting that tool to his hand. According to *Fortune*'s sampling, which is detailed in a later chapter, 85 percent of these men graduated from college, one out of three of them with academic honors. Of the college graduates, over 40 percent went on to take graduate degrees. Nor was their education wholly a gift from God or parent: 80 percent of these men worked to pay for some part of its cost. One out of three of them went to school at night. And the few men in the group who never went beyond high school set about teaching themselves, with such dedicated ferocity that they now face with equanimity the men with the doctorates. As a group, these men are the best-educated ever to emerge in positions of business importance. And, significantly enough, most of them spent at least some portion of their academic lives in a study of the useful disciplines, like engineering or economics or accounting. Their education served to arm them for some kind of business activity.

Thus armed, they entered the business world. Generally speaking, they entered it in the employ of a big company. And in that big company environment—that natural habitat where their business life began—they have remained ever since. They may have changed companies, and they almost certainly have changed jobs, but they never spent very much time during their mature life in the employ of a small business. What the community is to the characters in the novels of William Faulkner, the big organization became to the young executives: the natural field for their action. It is their kind of society.

As soon as these men were educated and plunged into corporate life, they began to display still more common attitudes and traits of character. Business not only occupied them, it preoccupied them. They wove business into the very fabric of their lives. Whether the objective of their attention was New Hampshire hemp or Chilean copper, they presently became devoted to it, and that devotion has never flagged. They are never flippant or cynical about their business, and they never question whether the game is worth the candle. They do not share the view of one advertising man, who confesses that "the trouble with me is that in the last analysis I just don't *care* about the toothpaste." The young executives are not plagued by doubts like that. They care. They always have.

Consequently, caring so much, they have always been clambering up the learning tree. To learn, and then learn more —that process has become a kind of article of faith that all these men embrace. "I learned something from that" is the young man's universal comment about every business experience, fortunate or unfortunate, that he has been through. He believes in experience as a teacher, and he has the dispassionate, analytic kind of mind that enables him to profit from it. When he scores a business triumph, he is gratified, but he does not spend much time in self-congratulation—he is busy, instead, sorting out and studying the reasons behind the victory. When something goes wrong, he subjects the events to the same kind of disinterested review, and if he discovers himself to have been at fault he coolly tucks away for future use as much as he can find out about what caused him to err. It becomes one kind of error he won't make again. To recriminate with himself or be tortured by guilt feelings over mistakes would be totally out of character for him. Mistakes are part of the learning process. "When I lose," says one man, "I just try to benefit from it for the next go-round."

To change, which is the one constant that they all confront, they usually respond in the same way. They are all habituated to change: no element in their "problem"—their favorite word to describe any business situation, good or bad, that they are coping with—has ever remained the same for very long. Sarape-wrapped Indians from Central America score a sudden song hit, or an oil well is spudded in near Bengazi, and the young executives have a new situation to manage. To a man, they all begin by spading up all the relevant facts—from "Where are the Indians now?" and "What songs of theirs have we already taped?" to "What is the specific gravity of that crude?"—and they want those facts in mint condition. One man is so keen on this point that he grumbles about his computer, complaining that "all it can give me is historical data." Then, to a man, they will compare and evaluate and test their beloved facts. They subscribe, all unknowing, to the judgment of Learned Hand: "We have no warrant of assurance save by everlasting readiness to test, and test again," and that everlasting process holds eternal fascination for them.

But since they know facts so well, they also know the limitations of fact. By now they have reached the level of managerial responsibility where facts can only tilt a man in the direction of his decision; they cannot lead him unerringly to it. So in comes another common quality these men are positively imbued with: confidence. They are dealing with problems that have long tentacles; the young men know that their solution may be wrong. Again all unknowing, they have heeded the cry of Oliver Cromwell to the Assembly of the Church of Scotland: "I beseech you . . . think it possible you may be mistaken." But they angle the thought inward instead of outward: "You can only be right fifty percent of the time anyway," they say.

Accepting that truth, the young man genuflects to the powers of darkness, and then makes his decision, as one of them says, "in that immeasurable area where things and people meet." He is full of confidence in his own intuitive powers of decision-making. And, for all his willingness to admit that he may be wrong, he remains quite certain that no one else, sitting where he sits, could be right more often. "I'm just egotistical enough," says one manager grimly, "to think that I can do this job better than anybody else they've got around here." That is a conviction which the young executive continually expresses now; he may express it less, later on in his career, when someone else, and not he, is selected to be chief executive. But it seems unlikely, no matter how little he voices the conviction in the future, that he will ever cease to believe it. It is a beam that supports too large a section of his personality ever to be removed.

To suggest that the conviction could weaken would be to admit that the young man may be beaten in fair competition. He concedes that this could happen, but he regards it as only the barest of possibilities. He is accustomed to winning—largely because he competes so fiercely to win. He competes everywhere: on the golf course ("I play to win"), in sibling rivalry against other people in his company, against outside companies, and even against the great abstractions like defeat or despair. He will struggle to win, and sacrifice to win, and find happiness when he wins—and then gather himself together to compete once more. He competes in a way that is always grim and hard, that may become bitter at times. He is so competitively constructed that he needs no specific enemy to stimulate him: as casually as though he were naming the competitor across the street, one young man identifies the enemy as "stupidity and ignorance, I guess"—and then throws himself with gusto into the fight. Competition is his meat and drink. And the organization, of course, supplies the arena within which the competition takes place.

In the young executive's catechism, work is a basic tenet. "I just work harder than anybody else around here," he says, unaware that his voice is but one in a chorus sounding the same note. Just why he works so hard is not easy to determine: motivation is a compound, pestled of many elements, and no single impulse drives these men to work the way they do. Some of the motivating urge obviously comes from the wellsprings within the man, from the deepest fiber of his being. Some of it comes from his own professional standards. Externally, the organization plays a key role in motivating the man: it offers trophies that the young man spurs himself on to win, and it awards them in accordance with criteria that the man believes in and is nurtured by. All these motives interlace and interact, inciting the young executive to his strenuous efforts. Free in his judgments, he is tethered to his work.

The inner craving comes first. "I guess I've always had itchy britches," says one man, and he has lots of company in that respect. The typical young executive burns the office lights late at night, and mercilessly burns up that woodpile of energy he was born with, and he often says, in a favorite phrase, that he is doing it "for the good of the business." And he is. But more important, he is doing it to satiate a man within him, a howling man who provokes him to compete more, and accomplish more, and then to compete and accomplish more still. "If you're not particularly brilliant," says a U.S. Steel Executive, "then the man who is is going to beat you. How do you equalize it? The night work, lots of hours." Echoing the admonition of the businessman of fifty years ago, one young man says, "The only advice I ever give anyone is to keep grinding at the job" —a platitude to which they all append an endorsing amen.

To keep grinding at the job inevitably brings some familial conflicts. The young man is married, he lives in a comfortable house (average value: $37,000) and he has delighted statisticians by dandling 2.8 children on his knee—but not, apparently, for very long stretches of time. He spends an average of about five days out of every month away from home on business trips. He usually understands and commiserates with his wife when she cries, as one recently did, "But I don't understand *why* you have to go to St. Louis." Even though in this rather unusual instance the wife is well-informed about her husband's business problems ("She knows what metaglucoside is"), she had to be content with the reply: "Maybe I don't know why, either. But I have to go." And he always goes. Moreover, he often travels at night or over a weekend to get there. He may have heard his wife's wails of protest sympathetically enough; but they add up only to a feather on his scale of values. That leaves his wife probably bemused, and possibly infuriated. But she ends up by driving him to the airport anyway.

Sharpening this inner compulsion to work are self-imposed standards that the young executive is dedicated to. Although they may coincide with the standards prescribed by the organization, they exist independently of those. In part at least, they were inculcated in the man by his preparatory education, whether he got it in business school, in engineering school, or in specialized studies such as accounting. The young executive is a professional manager, a member of the society of professional managers who run the organization, who act in its name, and who feel their responsibility to that abstract but very real entity. From such a managerial brotherhood— whether the young executive is engineer, chemist, or lawyer— he has adopted standards of professional performance, and they complement his own inner urge. One business school graduate explains: "I want to do more than the boss requires. Satisfactory performance is simply not enough to suit me. I wish it were, I wish I could walk out of here at night and forget it, but I can't. The pressures get pretty heavy, and it's a lonely life sometimes—I can't unload the story of all the difficulties on my wife, she's taking care of the kids, she wants to talk about her own problems. But I can't make myself take the attitude that 'it's just a job, and I do what I can.' My basic drive is for excellence—the standard I want to meet."

Another young executive embroiders on this theme. "My boss says, 'I'm not forcing you to do this,' " he confesses. "He says, 'Don't come in tomorrow.' But I *have* to come in. I would even if I had a rich uncle. People say, 'Don't bring your briefcase home.' But I *have* to. Sometimes I wake up at 5:00 A.M., and think of something, and I'll go downstairs and work at it. Then I can't get back to sleep. Or maybe we come home late on Friday night. I pick up my work, instead of a magazine. On vacation, I'm unhappy. On the beach, I walk over to a guy, and find out what he does, and we talk business, and I enjoy myself for three hours or so. The rest of the time I'm bored. I like to work, I like to see my ideas come forward." Then he adds with some embarrassment: "That's my problem."

The young man knows that he could give the organization less and survive within its ranks. But the knowledge does not diminish his own efforts as a professional. "I know guys who actually just hole up around here," says one electronics engineer. "They retire at forty—and continue to draw their pay. I could probably do the same thing, but I won't." Another agrees: "Sure, the security-seeker category exists. But to me, it isn't security—it's bondage." Another has remarked that "many hide within the system." And some blame the system for allowing that to happen: "Some of these companies, and I'm afraid this is one of them, only get about 50 percent out of a man," one young executive complains. "He's got another 50 percent that he may be willing to give, but he holds it back. He doesn't know how to give it, he's afraid of top management, he's taking a risk, or so he thinks, when he suggests a change. He doesn't want to stick his neck out, so he keeps doing it the old way, although he's sure he knows a better way. A procurement man who works for me should have more responsibility in buying . . . he wants it, he's good at it, and he ought to have it. But he won't go up to our boss and say so. He doesn't think he could do himself anything but harm if he tried."

The organization man may have been the archetype of such timid and fearful men, whose objective is merely to ride out the balance of their careers undiscovered and undisturbed. Insofar as he was that, the organization man probably still exists, and probably in considerable numbers. But mistakes come with the assumption that this man, who never sheds his protective coloration, is the most important inhabitant of the corporate world. He isn't. Nor does he represent what the alert and effective organization wants to create: in fact it does not want to create him, it does not want to hire him, and it certainly does not promote him to important jobs. Instead, it looks for, hires, and promotes the young executives who come out of a very different mold. They are the men who recognize that they could probably work less. But they never consider anything for themselves except working more.

One of them, who was under extraordinary pressure, related when this study began that he was sure his work load would lessen someday. That is not an unusual opinion to hear from young executives. When the same man was interviewed again recently, over a year after the first discussion, he was reminded of his previous hope that the burden of work by now would begin to ease up a little. He looked somewhat surprised at the reminder. Then he said slowly: "Well, things are pretty much the same around here." Really, this man, like so many of his associates, knows within himself that the happier day will never come. Indeed, for him it would not be a happier day, but a miserable one.

Another young executive emphasized that he is working mostly in order to develop people, and when he has made them capable of the kind of performance he wants, he himself will start to work less hard. But he too really knows better: first of all, his subordinates will never be able to reach the degree of perfection that he urges on them. He is constantly raising his own standards of what he expects—of himself, but of them as well—as their performance improves, and the goal will be always retreating out of reach. Second, when he has around him people who can do more of the kind of work that he is now doing himself, he will simply open new doors for his own efforts: he will move into different expanses, refine and refine, improve and improve, in an endless uncoiling of effort. His basic psychological construction is such that he could never make his own applications of energy less diligent. At bottom, most of the young executives know this; some are simply more willing to admit it to themselves and to their wives than others are. "There's no question about whether I want a job where I could make more money and work less," comments one young executive with General Electric. "That's clear. I don't. I hope the day never comes when I don't work hard." All of them more or less secretly agree.

In the ganglia of the young executive's motivations, the organization plays a critical role. He is not motivated by the organization to don the armor of corporate thought and corporate mores, or to submit silently to some mystic kind of general will. It would not suit the larger purposes of the organization for him to do those things. Instead, the organization, if it is a good one, urges him to greater individual efforts by providing the trophies that it knows he cherishes: the ones that symbolize triumphs, and so gratify the executive's inner drives —what W. Lloyd Warner has described as his "high achievement desires."

Thus the organization holds up before the young man's eyes a clutch of silver cups that he can win. Among them, money, status, and promotions—and the added responsibilities that promotions bring—glitter most brightly. The company, besides offering the prizes, is also the arbiter and the judge. It makes some rules, and it supplies the norms by which the effectiveness of the young executive's actions can be determined. It hangs up scoreboards by which this competitive man can keep track of his performance and compare it with the performance of his colleagues. The profit-and-loss statements of section and division, and the consolidated per-share earnings of the company, give him a convenient map on which to plot out the results of his work.

To these varied stimuli, the young man reacts in various ways. To make money is certainly a compelling force with him. But it is rarely the dominating one. Already these men are earning well: annual salaries are complicated by retirement and pension plans, as well as stock options and profit-sharing, but the low end of the salary scale for these men seems to run around $20,000 a year, and it ranges up to $75,000 or more for the older members of the group. The young executive, however, is far from rich: the average group member calculates his net worth at $49,000. "Ever know anybody who didn't want more?" he usually asks.

But the fact is that after a certain point salary increases cease to move him very much, especially in view of what the tax laws do to them. Obviously, much more enthusiasm is generated about stock options than about salary raises. Yet simply to earn more money is not the only reason that this man makes those strenuous extra efforts—at least, not to make more money for its own sake. Money takes on more importance largely for the reason that Max Weber recognized a long time ago: it remains a proof of the successful fulfillment of duty, and evidence that the young executive has found the social position to which his merits entitle him. There is an obvious relationship between money and success, especially in the corporate world: academicians, doctors, and scientists can have their success rewarded in other ways as well, but among businessmen money remains the most widely accepted success symbol. That gives it a relative, rather than an absolute, importance: the young executive is liable to express his greatest interest in salary when there is somehow disclosed to him that most secretly held bit of corporate information, the salary of a colleague. Then all his competitive instincts are aroused. But as for what money can buy the young executive—that has its importance, but after certain needs are met it is not the overwhelming single motivation that Vance Packard and others have assumed it to be. Strong, perhaps, but still typical are the responses of one young executive on the matter: "Money? What am I going to do with it? What's the point? We live well, all my children are being well educated, we've got everything we need already. I've already got one Corvette—so who wants two?" Another adds: "I just haven't got the yacht mentality."

Neither does he have much of the stockholder mentality. That white-haired old lady in sneakers in whose stout defense members of top management speak so vehemently and so often is a comparative stranger to the young executives. They leave her fate to the boss: she seems to them neither very real nor very close. To the boss, of course, the stockholder appropriately enough is a continual concern: one president of a huge U.S. corporation talks constantly about the pressure stockholders put on him: "The burden is laid on me by the stockholders and the board," says this chief executive. "It comes pressing down hard on me and on top management. We try to transmit some of that pressure to the upper middle ranks of management. At the same time, though, those ranks are being pressured from below, from the plants and the divisions —pressures from the immediate operating problems, the specific situations of production, distribution and sales. The two pressures meet, they flow together you might say, at the upper middle section of corporate life"—in other words, at the level now occupied by the young executives.

But the young executives really make only formal obeisance to the pressure from above. They do refer to the stockholder occasionally, but only perfunctorily, and it is hard to conceive of them spending longer hours behind their desks for the stockholder's benefit. A similar removed quality attaches to their views about their companies' per-share earnings. Like the white-haired widow, consolidated profits belong to the realm of the boss' concern. Of course such views are not held by every member of the group, the ones who are closer to top management obviously being more immediately involved—but generally speaking, while the young executives care about the stockholder and the company's total performance, they do not go to the office on Saturdays for the stockholder's sake.

The performance of the division under the young executive's hand is quite a different matter. Its scoreboard provides him with a tangible criterion by which to determine whether he is meeting his own standard of excellence. So he battles for point after point on that scoreboard, in that way satisfying both his company and himself. And, as a collateral gain, by scoring well he wins the respect of his fellows in the professional brotherhood. The score may be invisible to outsiders, but the man's colleagues in the company and his professional partners in the brotherhood can read and admire what the scoreboard says. To the world at large, of course, the young executive's successes, the results perhaps of a series of innovations over a long period of time, are invisible—imparting to him an anonymity that he may rebel against in later life. But for the present he is undisturbed. "What we do is unrecognized by the great American public, but who cares?" asks one manager. "I prefer recognition in the company. It's nice when the president says, 'Pretty good.' "

But promotions are what hold real magic for him. They are the invisible sprigs of laurel that he cherishes. They constitute what Adolph Berle has called "the transcendental margin" in this man's life. Promotions carry with them those twin excitements, "more challenge and more responsibility," and toward those goals he drives with real ferocity. As he wins a larger share of them, one need is submerged, a higher need emerges, and the man presses on to gratify that new need. The basic requirements of life are met, but motivation remains strong, and psychic expectations are enlarged. The boredom that afflicted the elite social groups of earlier epochs is banished forever, for, as A. H. Maslow wrote, "What is boredom, after all, but over-gratification." By pressing forever forward, the young executive, who corresponds to Maslow's "self-actualizing person," can feed the howling man within. He is his own hard taskmaster.

Necessarily, there is another side which complements that kind of confidence and drive. The point has been exaggerated, but it remains nonetheless true that the horrendous thought of failure also whips up the young executive to seek promotion. There is a monkey on his back, and the ride can get pretty rough for the young manager—maybe intolerably rough— when the promotions start going to someone else.

Sometimes, the young executive's objectivity and forbearance—both qualities he has consciously developed as business aids—can save him under those circumstances. "There was this big job opening in Chicago," one man recalls. "I thought I was the one for it. Then I got a call from a vice-president, explaining why they had picked someone else who was older. I was and I am the better man. But I was told that this other man's abilities would have been lost to our company if they hadn't picked him. At the end of the conversation I said to the vice-president, 'All right.' He said, 'Aren't you even going to argue?' I said, 'I can't argue—you're right.' It was a great personal disappointment to me." But the ending in the case is happy: "That vice-president went to the executive vice-president and told him my reaction. The executive vice-president is now president, and the story has gone all over the company. I probably have gotten further by the reaction I showed than if I had been given the job in the first place." Yet under different circumstances, where a young executive may see the chances for promotions slipping away, he may begin to entertain a hunted feeling—his burrowed inner self, that same howling man, becoming the hunter.

But while he is making progress through corporate ranks, he finds the journey an important source of pleasure. And he works for that progress buoyed by the essential conviction that the business system metes out fair rewards to those who really give themselves to it. The young executive knows that there are tribulations and tests of fire to pass through. But in the end, so runs his belief, the system will reward the men who merit it, and those who don't—no matter what temporary gains they may enjoy—will soon level off. The cheater, the man who cuts corners, the one who lives off the abilities of others—they are many, but time will find them out. The system makes mistakes. It needs time to work its way out of them. But all the mistakes will be corrected when the final scenes are played. The young executive has spent years in the system, and he's done well; the system, in that sense, is good. He expects to do even better in the future—so he believes that the man who makes it to the top will deserve on his merits to have done so. The remark is banal, but one young executive voices it with real conviction: "If you try your best," he says, "right will prevail."

Linked to that faith in the system is a faith that progress can be achieved through the application of knowledge. Reason makes a difference in the external world; it can change things, improve conditions, burnish the present and save the future. Through reason, the earth can be civilized. (One is reminded, in these views, of *The Adventures of Caleb Williams* of 150 years ago.) Knowledge can move mountains. The man who said, "Ignorance is the enemy," spoke the certainty of his generation that through knowledge can come accomplishment—essentially, an optimistic conviction which ties the young executive to the traditions of the Western world as they emerged from the Renaissance. But the young executive doesn't know that, being largely ignorant of the Renaissance: he did not acquire his optimistic faith in the usefulness of knowledge through any such esoteric means as reading about the period.

It came to him empirically, out of his own experience. Viewed whole, his is the experience of the generation of Americans whose mature lives began with the end of World War II. That generation, to which most of the young executives belong, has never had more than a brush with a real defeat, has never been ground down by poverty, or oppressed by the garrison state. The young executive, this hard-surfaced man so well equipped to cope with modern conditions, has never been caught in a situation so crushing and overpowering that his own efforts became futile or pathetic. He may have some childhood recollection of the Depression, but he is not the depression's child, for he never had to struggle with it hand-to-hand. He has never suffered over the prospect of a sharp reduction in his fortunes or circumstances. "I don't think any of us worry about unemployment," says one man in behalf of his generation. Such anxieties are beyond his ken. If his company were hard hit, about the worst that he can see happening to him is that he might stop being promoted for a while—and even that concern seems a bit unreal to him. To move onward and upward—to progress by the hard application of his knowledge—is a commonplace of his experience.

Thus pragmatism becomes his guiding philosophy. The

whole significance of his business life he measures by his effectiveness in the world outside, that external world of people, products, and problems that he moves in. For him, thought is an analytic activity that leads to action in a concrete situation, that supplies a solution to the concrete business problem that comes before him at a given moment in time. In the words of one manager, his business function is "to create a thought, to think up a plan, to think out the ramifications, and then"—now comes the universal emphasis—"to bring it into being, to sit back and say, 'It's working.'" Once that is done, he can go on to a new creation, and start that working too—in a never-ending process of refinement and improvement. His job is like the river that Heraclitus looked at so speculatively: it is never the same from one hour to another, and on its flux he can impose his formulae, his practical solutions that create new problems that require new applications of his highly applicable kind of causality, and he has considerable talent in devising his solutions.

Listen to Them Talk

Competent, technically trained, and experienced, the young executive is often the object of attention from executive-search firms. He often assesses, therefore, where he stands with his company, and what it would take to tempt him away from it. Does he feel too much at peace with his organization ever to leave it? If he does leave, does he always go where the money is?

An engineer, age thirty-seven: *"I've got calls from executive-search people. I've had offers of more money. But it would have to involve something more than money for me. Something would have to go awfully wrong with my present job. I think writers on the subject underestimate the extent of a man's commitment to his company. But don't get the idea that I'm fat and happy and satisfied. I don't feel like rushing out to another company, but that doesn't mean I'm complacent. The kind of work I'm doing, what I know, just isn't the kind of commodity you can go out and sell at a hot-dog stand.*

"*Most of the stuff you read about executives and their lives is downright wrong. It's hogwash. Oh, I have been told by the boss once in a while to go out and look at this and prove it's right, I get a little of that. But usually I have freedom to direct efforts on my own ideas. The last proposal I presented to our executive vice-president—he said he would rather have cyanide in his coffee than hear about it. But when he was shown, he was receptive. As it turned out, we made it work. We picked up and sold a few things that my predecessor couldn't handle, not because we're any smarter than he was but because we're new, I think my job has been change. I'm supposed to initiate change. But you can't stay on a job like that too long; you do better if you're new at it.*"

A systems engineer, age forty-one: "*I've never really considered leaving. I've been with this company sixteen years, and it would take a good deal of money and security to get me—a good deal more than just a $10,000-a-year increase. Before you reach a certain salary level, money is the important thing. After that, job satisfaction takes over. We all know that some companies will pay you a lot for two or three years just to get what you know, and then let you go.*

"*I've only been on this assignment a year. I feel I haven't mastered it yet. I have my troubles. Sometimes I get caught up in the conflict between line and staff. The staff man is not always welcome, I know. He has a closer tie to the vice president. Line people are afraid that what they say to the staff man may get to the vice-president.*

"*Everyone aspires, certainly. When I've mastered this job, I hope to move off of it to another one. I can see a goal, yes—a job I want. There are fifteen of them in the company now; I can't imagine being blocked. I've moved four times for this company in the past eight years. A good way to get stymied is to say 'I don't want to move.'*"

The young executive has never worked anywhere except for a big company. Did he choose it because it offered him a haven? Has he found it easy? Does he want to go only where it is easier still?

A production manager, age thirty-two: "*What's the price of a man? In my case, I knew right from the time I first took a job that I would go with some large corporation or other. There's appeal in something that is large, but it has nothing to do with security. The buccaneer versus the peace and security of big business—the choice never presented itself to me that way. Now I've been with this company six years, and after you've been in big business for a while, the thought of owning your own company becomes intriguing. But it's a nebulous kind of thought. It would take a remarkable opportunity, the sudden realization that here was a crying need and you had the wherewithal to supply it. It would be your own show, and your profits—plus the intrigue of building something.*

"Or if I had a deep conviction that I was barred forever from the top job with this company, then I might leave. But being blocked by old Joe, the guy just ahead of me? I don't worry about that, I could get around old Joe. And I don't worry about money, because money follows with advancement. I'd like more money, but it doesn't eat at me. If jobs and salary are inverse, the higher you go the less salary, I admit I don't think I'd be so interested.

"On my present job, I have plenty of opportunity to make my own decisions. Still, I would like to be less restrained. There's always an environment of policy that's peculiar to a company, partly from the character of its stockholders. Stockholders hold our company stock for revenue. The board of directors and our strong management make their feelings known. If I happened to be a devotee of wild-eyed growth, presumably profitable eventually, this point of view would be hard to sell in my company. If it were my own business, I could go ahead. These restraints are not the ulcer-producing, stomach-wrenching type. They're only reasons why I might go into my own business someday."

A company vice-president, age forty-three: *"I don't have any degrees. I started at Amherst, then it was wartime, and by the end of the war I had a wife and two kids—that ended the education. I don't think I ever had a tremendous thirst for the intellectual life. I'm doing better than I thought I'd be doing at this stage in life, to be honest. I wonder how salable I am to somebody else . . . God knows who'd want me.*

'At the mill, the thing I miss most is somebody who has an idea about how to do things better. I'm always glad to hear about a better way. . . . It's hard to know what you're doing wrong, and the guy who will let you know what is going on, and what the criticisms are, is welcome.

"But I wouldn't leave my company now. We've gone through a long corporate struggle. If I were going to leave, I would have left at the beginning of it. Now I've gone through so much of it that I wouldn't want to walk out. It's been very painful at times. And now there's this guy who could block me. But until the whole corporate thing gets straightened out, I don't know what's going to happen. All I know is that I've got to stay around to find out."

Chapter THREE

The Man and the House He Does Not Enter

For all the talents that the young executive can show in solving his business problems, however, his intelligence has limitations. There are fields beyond its frontiers, fields rich with personal rewards, that his intelligence does not enter. His intellect is narrow in range and, although it can burn brightly, its focus is very sharp; there is no diffusion into the broader areas of learning. To outsiders, this limitation imparts a kind of incompleteness to the man.

All his business efforts are of course intellectual. (Surprisingly, many academicians do not seem to assign him even that much credit, since they appear to be reluctant to equate success in business with repeatedly successful strokes of the intellect.) But the intellectual quality of the young executive's efforts has a single-purposed and penetratingly practical cast to it. It is as though his intellect were shaped to fit business conditions, created to solve business problems, marvelously capable of registering and recording and acting on the facts of business—but somehow unsuited to other intellectual pursuits. His mind has independence and strength and capacity, but it leaves him where he is all too willing to be left, far from certain kinds of intellectual pleasures—and often they are the very kind which, were he able to engage in them, would bring him personal benefits and would make him more appealing as a figure in society.

Foremost among those pleasures are the very keen and very

satisfying rewards that can come from some pursuit of the humanities and the liberal arts. That is an area where the mind of the young executive rarely roams.

During the business day, of course, there is no time and not much occasion for that activity. "There just isn't the time," one young executive points out, "or the place in the business of running a large corporation to preach the gospel of interest in the humanities. Corporate executives have to get the job done. It's rare to be able to take a couple of weeks off. And when you can, you probably want to go back to professional school, to catch up."

Nor does the young executive by volition practice the disciplines of the liberal arts in his leisure hours. For one thing, those "leisure hours" are far fewer in number than the ones he is assumed to have: work at home, brought bulging in a briefcase, cuts deeply into leisure time. When he reads in the evenings, he is likely to read business reports and trade journals: one young executive out of three, according to *Fortune*'s survey, dedicates all of his "leisure reading" to subjects directly pertinent to his office work. Where the young executive does read books unrelated to his business, they are mostly the superficial and easy kind: Ian Fleming is a prime example. Or he leans toward the current best-sellers of the lower quality.

Many of his other leisure activities have a nonintellectual and even an anti-intellectual character. It is as though, being drained of mental energy by his job, he deliberately turned his back on the kind of cultural activities that requires a flex of the intellectual muscles. So he plays golf at Happy Knoll, and talks over what happened in the locker room—a side of himself that lends itself all too readily to caricature, and that has often been taken for the whole extra-office man. Hunting and fishing are also favorite activities, sometimes carried out and discussed at such length and with such eagerness as to permit the inference that they are pastimes chosen and treasured precisely because they are so devoid of intellectual content.

Culturally, of course, these extracurricular habits make the young executive a narrow man. To him, speculative thought is as foreign as the game of *bocce:* it belongs to another culture, which he neither understands nor has any curiosity about. His own propensity for action makes speculation a far-off, even an idle pursuit. He is not likely to understand ideas that are not useful or applicable, and he may not care much about an abstract or abstruse quest for understanding in the speculative realm. If he was on a college campus in the 1940's, as many of these men were, he probably took a survey course in philosophy as a freshman, sighed with relief when he passed it, and dismissed it from his mind—swinging his intellectual headlamp toward something that mattered, that could make a visible difference, a visible change.

Thus the blind spot gapes. Like some scientists, the young executive has little interest in, and less understanding of, the liberal arts. In an academic sense, the young executive does not know what the humanities are. He has no grasp of good literature, and no understanding of the discipline of aesthetics. He has probably not mentioned Keats since he left high school. He does not care, in the phrase of Charles Grosvenor Osgood, to investigate "the operations of the grand laws and mysterious forces that dominate every age: of will and liberty, of pain and retribution and justice, of love and sacrifice. . . ." He does not appreciate works of the imagination. He has never heard the music of the spheres. He would not recognize it if he did. And he could not care less, because, to use the currently popular jargon, he is completely "job oriented" and "result oriented."

That the young executive is deficient in that way is not entirely his fault. If he is a kind of technological illiterate—and in a few cases that may not be going too far, as long as "technological" means the whole technology of business—the condition results from what the late A. Whitney Griswold called "the ancient conflict between two kinds of learning"—broadly, the vocational kind and the liberal arts kind—that took place some years ago at the high school level in the United States.

In that conflict, Griswold says, "liberal education lost ground by default. . . . The sad part of it is that what began as an involuntary and almost imperceptible schism culminated in an acrimony and a second Battle of the Books. It is not necessary to become embroiled in the battle to recognize the harmful effect of this dissidence on liberal education. . . . What should have been a colloquium turned into a conflict in which no one gained and liberal education was the heavy loser." Griswold found that liberal arts studies "are disappearing under a layer of vocational and other substitutes like the landscape in the ice age, only this glacier reaches from coast to coast and from border to border." And the disappearance, to Griswold, would mean the loss of the real purpose of the liberal arts: "To awaken and develop the intellectual and spiritual powers of the individual before he enters upon his chosen career, so that he may bring to that career the greatest possible assets of intelligence, resourcefulness, judgment and character."

Griswold wrote those words about ten years ago; much has changed since then, and the "ancient conflict" may not now be so bitterly fought as it was in the 1950's. But the point is that most of the young executives got an important part of their education while the conflict was at its height. And most of them stood with the "practical men"—notably, with the engineers.

Many businessmen—but significantly enough, more of the older ones than the younger—protest against this description of the young executives as incomplete men. They offer two main arguments in rebuttal. First, that the young businessman is active in the cultural life of his community, helping in the sponsorship of symphony orchestras, opera houses, and other cultural groups. The second argument takes this direction: that the study of the humanities in the end is the study of humanity, the study of people; that the young executives, technically educated or not, must cope constantly with people, and therefore, as Joseph Wilson, president of Xerox, says, "Businessmen must be involved with the humanities . . . the capacity to communicate, to persuade, to inspire are among the most important attributes a businessman can have. I don't know where you get that capacity except from the humanities. If profit alone were the objective, we could get that by shooting dice. But in rendering a service, you inspire people with ideals, you articulate the effort so that it runs smoothly. You must have a sense of duty. I don't know where you get that, either, if not from the humanities."

Yet such arguments are not telling. The organization and support of the symphony orchestra, the successful rescue of a failing opera house or an art gallery, are really undertaken by the young executive (if he does undertake it) largely as a business function. It comes down, in the end, to doing what he knows about: figuring costs, estimating income, bridging the gap, selling and promoting. It is not an activity accomplished as a cultural exercise, but more as a business sideline, as a kind of leisure-time push-up by a man who does push-ups all day long for a living. It helps to have that busman's holiday thought of as a cultural pursuit, and the man carrying it out in all honesty may think of it that way too. But as a function, it remains in the active, doer realm. Sponsorship of a symphony orchestra is a qualitatively different pursuit than, say, an interest in Mozart; the proper arrangement of a safe shipment of valuable paintings is different from an appreciation of art.* None of this is intended to mean, obviously, that there are no Mozart lovers or ardent scrutinizers of painting to be found among the young executive group. Doubtless there are some. But not very many.

To call the young executive's negotiations with people a humanistic activity is to commit another kind of error. These managers do deal with people all day long—at their level of management, people, rather than plants or products, are sure to take up most of the executive's time. But the people are there, in the favorite word of the young executive himself, to be "motivated" and to be manipulated. They exist in the young executive view as part of the business problem, perhaps the most important part: they are people whose resistance is to be overcome, their talents fully realized, their hardest efforts elicited, and their rewards made commensurate with their performance, all for the purpose, again in the managerial vocabulary, of "getting the job done." The necessary and perfectly respectable and praiseworthy objective of the manager is to get the most out of his people.

Nothing cruel or heartless need be read into that purpose. There is no indication whatever that young executives as we have defined them are any whit less sympathetic to people, or any less kind to their mothers, than any other members of the human race. But even if we assume that they are more warmhearted, generous, and lovable than other members—and that seems unlikely—that only makes them good humanitarians and decent people, not good humanists. They can get their "capacity to persuade," to revert to Mr. Wilson's phrase, from many other sources besides a study of the humanities. They can get their sense of duty just as easily from other quarters. Soldiers do. Doctors and lawyers do. And so can businessmen.

Writing in *Fortune* a few years ago, Louis Finkelstein decided that "the modern business leader is more often than not bewildered at the suggestion that the future of the Republic is in some way related to the ideas and ideals of John Locke, not to mention Spinoza and the medieval scholastics." In agreement, Russell Kirk, also in *Fortune,* stated that the business-

* The current disputes over the operation of New York's temple of culture, Lincoln Center, buttress the point. Perhaps the lesson there is not so much that business and art cannot understand each other as that temples of culture ought not to be built in the first place.

men "are deficient in the disciplines that nurture the spirit.
. . . They are largely ignorant of the humanities, that great
body of literature that records the wisdom of the ages. People
can live on their moral and intellectual capital for a long time,
yet eventually unless the capital is replenished they arrive at
cultural bankruptcy, and the result of such bankruptcy is a
society of meaninglessness."

But Kirk then went to less secure ground. "Even if the humanities are chiefly important for a man's soul and the higher
purposes of life," he wrote, "they are good for profits too.
. . . The sheer variety of ideas that the liberal arts man has
explored can be counted on to give him a resourcefulness generally superior to the man who has only technical training."

Unfortunately, there is considerable doubt that they can be
counted on to do any such thing. The point smacks of Dale
Carnegie—the humanistic disciplines, it seems to say, can pay
off in the business world. The trouble with the point is that it
overlooks the fact that the young executive, technically trained
or not, has plenty of on-the-job ideas and resourcefulness. If
the managerial task is knitting together and directing various
technical efforts, as it so often is, some technical understanding to begin with is very important. There is no evidence that
the liberal arts man could do the young executive's job better
than the present incumbent. It seems a safer bet, as a matter of
fact, that he could not do it as well.

The question is, then, how much importance should be at-
tached to the fact that the young executive has this blind side?
Does it really make any difference, after all? Reverting to the
rather extreme illustration, to read Keats affords a qualitatively different and higher kind of pleasure than to read Ian
Fleming, but the choice of pleasures, as the reader of Keats
would be first to say, must lie with the individual. The real
question is whether the interests of the business community,
and therefore ultimately of our society, will suffer from the
young executive's "result orientation."

In some ways it may. There is no easy answer, but the time
will come when the young executive sets his company policy
on broad social and economic matters. When it does, how
good will he be at the job?

In many ways, he has broader business views, and broader
social views too, than the preceding generation. He is less out
of step with society, surely, than the president of the National
Association of Manufacturers was in 1926, when he said, "The
five-day week is an unworthy ideal . . . it is better not to

trifle with God's laws." And he is less out of step than a different president of the same organization who remarked almost forty years later, "Some of my best friends are intellectuals."

Some of that increase in breadth of vision comes from the young executive's own intelligent view of his company's function. To the word "profit," for example—still an epithet in some circles—the young executive gives a wide and wise definition. He regards profit as the supplier of the only sensible basis on which business can be conducted. And he is capable also of thinking not only of profits today, but also of profits in the future. As well as he can, he weighs with his decisions on immediate questions the considerations of the long-range interests of his company—a kind of wisdom not usually associated with the buccaneers of another age.

His belief in profit—profit interpreted judiciously—as a basic tenet makes it possible for him to avoid some conflicts that might have a paralyzing effect on his function as a manager. He sees no clash between profit and social responsibility as concepts, thus avoiding the popular error of books like *Executive Suite,* which suggested that good works should motivate a company, and *Man in the Gray Flannel Suit,* whose hero renounced business values—but who conveniently ended up by inheriting a fortune. With sensible pragmatism, the young executive makes his decisions without heeding the cautions that one management book says he should be mindful of: "What will this decision mean in terms of the standard of living of the American people? . . . Does it promote economic stability? Is it good for personal security? Does it help preserve order? Is it just?" He knows the impossibility of folding into an already difficult decision such ingredients as those.

Yet he is conscious of ethical overtones to his work. Writing on the question in *Social Responsibilities of the Businessman,* Howard Bowen found that "Within the past few years, large numbers of businessmen have publicly acknowledged and actively preached the doctrine that . . . management in the interests of the stockholders only is not the sole end of their duties. An increasing number of businessmen are beginning to regard management as a profession having similar underlying ethical principles and social responsibilities as medicine or the law."

To pass judgment on ethical standards is highly difficult. An endeavor to show that the young executive has higher ethical standards than, say, the business buccaneers of fifty years ago would turn out to be a very complicated and probably a fruitless undertaking. The specific needs of the times always play a part in determining the standards of ethics; so do other personal and organizational elements hard to weigh.

But it seems safe to say about the young executive that he is mindful of the existence of ethical questions, and conscious of their difficulty, and, generally, anxious to avoid conduct that would be regarded as contrary to the interests of the business community, and therefore unbusinesslike. He does not face decisions that have a high ethical content very often, since most such decisions fall in the purview of top management: 40 percent of the young executives who responded to *Fortune*'s question said that they "almost never" were confronted with business decisions that also involved ethical issues. But when such issues do come up, the young executive is apt to try to see them whole, with an understanding that his own standards are involved, and so is his loyalty to the company; and he is apt to be able to grasp the special complexity and compounded difficulty such questions acquire when he must act not in his own name but in the name of the organization. He does not appear to need the liberal arts to help him in this.

He has also progressed in his views about the image of business in the public mind. Like his precursors, the young executive regards himself as widely misunderstood by the public at large. He believes that public opinion is shot through with mistaken economic ideas and mistaken notions of what business is all about. Those notions, he thinks, result in equally mistaken judgments about the merits of business, judgments which diminish his own importance and the importance of his company and the business community at large. But he has not been driven by such beliefs, as some of his predecessors were, into any "the public be damned" attitude. He is clearly too sophisticated for that.

But he is less clear in his views of how to correct the misimpressions. Some of the resentments against "big business," the young executive believes, might subside if more facts about its true processes were known. He knows very well—no one knows better—that the facts are stubborn and complicated; he knows that they are hard to explain, and he doubts that many people want to take the trouble to listen. (Once the young executive himself is assured that the listener is genuinely interested—an experience he does not often have outside the business community—he talks avidly and earnestly; in a sense, that eagerness reflects his belief that most people are indifferent to his work.) If they did listen, though—so runs the young executive's reasoning—some current misconceptions would be dissipated. More people would probably end up, as he has, by accepting the aims and goals of the business community, and fully appreciating their importance. From time to time, he makes himself what Howard Bowen calls "the torchbearer of economic literacy," taking unto himself an educational function; at other times, he is inclined simply to accept the fact that he is likely to be misunderstood, and push ahead anyway.

On the whole, though, his approach to the problem, while not clearly worked out, would probably favor putting more of the difficult facts on the public table than have ever been available before. He believes that it is hard, perhaps impossible, to correct what is wrong by mere manipulation. He thinks that more will be required to improve the image of business than the exercise of "public relations" if that phrase means a maneuvering of public thought. And he also senses correctly that more is needed than "a simple matter of meeting the folks," as a corporation president put it a few years ago. The young executive is suspicious and distrustful of such simple formulas. He would of course consult with the public relations department of his company on matters edging into the public domain; he would look for expert views on the subject from that department. And his own recommendation is likely to favor allowing the facts themselves to speak. It is a view that harmonizes with his general faith in the power of knowledge. It is hard to see how any conversance with the liberal arts could improve that view.

Yet it might. If the young executive could only bend that insatiable business curiosity of his toward society at large, he might learn more about the reasons for the public disfavor that sometimes touches business. Perhaps instead of thinking of himself as "a torchbearer of economic literacy," he might regard himself as a student of society, if only because the process of teaching by the businessman—even when the facts are heavily in his favor—does not appear ever to have been very efficacious. If he were more sensitive to social currents, if he understood them better—and it could be argued that such an understanding might come with a study of the liberal arts, which embrace the origins and the history of man's thought—he might come to know better why he and other businessmen are unpopular public figures. Somehow, that large question—that "why"—does not engage his interest. He never seems to have examined the point. He would probably say that he is too busy to do so.

So the young executive's understanding of the broad social context of business remains uncertain. Few businessmen are social leaders, and the young executive seems to have no more capacity for social leadership than his predecessors did. W. H. Whyte, Jr., pointed out ten years ago that the businessman was no longer in the forefront of the American dream, and the young executive today shows no signs of being able to put him there.

To judge from what seems to be happening on college campuses, the businessman begins to look instead like a character in an American nightmare. Teaching, research, law, and public service are taking precedence over business as careers. David Riesman in *The Lonely Crowd* found that the image of the businessman as a woefully dull "economic man" has made many undergraduates reluctant to undertake business careers. "Business is thought to be dull and disagreeable as well as morally suspect," Riesman wrote. "The notion that business today, especially big business, presents challenging intellectual problems and opportunities and is no more engaged in sharp practices than any other career, seems not to exist in the minds of students even whose fathers are businessmen."

Recent comments bear out Riesman's view. A lead item in the *Wall Street Journal* recently began with the sentence: "The word on the campus is that business is for the birds." The *Journal* went on to report the statement of an official of Amherst College that 48 percent of its alumni are businessmen, but fewer than 20 percent of recent graduates have been entering business. At Harvard—even with the nearby example of the prosperity being thrust on business school graduates—only 14 percent of the 1964 graduating class planned to enter business. The director of manpower development and training at the U. S. Chamber of Commerce told the *Journal*, "We are deeply concerned with the number of college youths who have rejected business as a career. We're worried about the poor attitude of many students toward business."

Continues the *Journal*: "One of the toughest obstacles confronting company recruiters on many campuses is a general atmosphere of scorn for business. It frequently drives potential executives and salesmen to choose other fields.

" 'Professors often cracked jokes implying that businessmen weren't very smart,' recalls a June graduate of Columbia. . . . 'Most students looked down on the student who said he was going into business.' . . . The image of the businessman and of corporate life found on the campus today is often highly unattractive—and, in the view of many executives, highly distorted. Students tend to look on the business world as a high-pressure, conformist place where superficial values prevail. . . . Many students view the businessman as 'preoccupied with thoughts of sales promotion and planned obsolescence, the man in the gray flannel suit with a martini and an ulcer, whose first responsibility is not his fellow man but his company's profits.' A 1964 Williams graduate, impeccably dressed in the collegiate uniform of conservative suit and button-down shirt, declares, 'The designs of your tie seem to make a lot of difference in business, and I just don't go for that.'

"College men frequently express fears that the business world would prove an intellectual Siberia. . . . An officer at Metropolitan Life Insurance Company recalls talking last year with an Indiana University graduate who 'spent more than half the interview seeking assurance that the work would be intellectually challenging.' "

It seems strange in some ways that the communication between the business world and the world of the college campus should be as bad as that. Many links obtain between the two spheres. The scientists and the Ph.D. holders in business are legion—especially working in the space industry, but elsewhere as well—and many of them teach courses or participate in some other active way in the academic life. And the role of the businessman—traditionally, a member of the board of directors—as university trustee is both familiar and important. And so are the contributions that the big companies make to education: The Esso Education Foundation, supported by Standard Oil of New Jersey and its domestic affiliates, granted $2,209,000 in 1963, and the effort was considered important enough so that each item was personally reviewed by Jersey's chief executive, Jack Rathbone, who served as a trustee of the foundation. And United States Steel, through its foundation, made a special contribution toward the humanities last year.

At Aspen, Colorado, a business-supported Institute for Humanistic Studies is working under the experienced direction of Alvin Eurich, formerly executive director of the Ford Foundation's education program and onetime president of the State University of New York. One of the institute's varied purposes is to increase the understanding between business and the humanities. The institute was begun by the efforts of a businessman—the late Walter Paepcke, president of the Container Corporation—and businessmen, such as the competent and affluent Robert Anderson of Roswell, New Mexico, now chief executive of the Atlantic Refining Co., still supply it with much of the vitality and money that carry it forward.

An *ad hoc* seminar at Aspen in 1964 was devoted to a discussion of the relations between business and the humanities. Present were two groups of academics—an Old Guard and a younger group, inevitably dubbed the Young Turks—and a group of businessmen. The discussion showed how much remains to be done before any real understanding emerges between business and the academy. At first, the academics themselves bogged down over a definition of the humanities, and were unable to agree whether the humanities were impoverished or flourishing. Then the educators, especially the younger ones who teach or participate in the creative arts, had the greatest trouble comprehending what the business world was all about, and what the businessmen present were saying. The confusion at times could hardly have been deeper.

The comments of some of the younger teachers illustrate the gulf between the groups. One young teacher of English, a vigorous defender of the humanities, remarked toward the end of the session, "I feel much closer to the scientists here than I do to any of the businessmen. The scientists and I understand each other. But when I meet businessmen, I'm meeting people who just don't talk the same language that I do. I wonder what we're doing sitting across from each other at the same table." Another teacher, after sitting through long sessions trying to determine what business owed the liberal arts and vice versa, took refuge in the view that the pleasure he experienced in the practice of his own humanistic discipline was quite sufficient justification for his life: "I teach an undergraduate course in art," he said. "It's a course about a very brief and special period five hundred years ago. I teach it because it gives me pleasure. That is quite enough reason. I think all one can hope for is that perhaps the businessman will view the humanities with a little more relaxation and with a little sense of fun."

A third young instructor decided to take advantage of the presence of businessmen to make a hardheaded pitch that he figured the hardheaded businessman could understand. "The humanities are desperately in need of money," he announced grimly. "With the population explosion there simply isn't enough money around. We need it badly at my university. Business does many things and offers many satisfactions to people in business, but the main satisfaction is to make money. The interest of the humanists in business is really an interest in the money that business has—an interest in your profits. You have these profits. Our message to you is—give us your profits. I won't say that we'll give you good novels or other things in return, because we may use your money to write a sad novel and then you might say you don't like it. So I just say—give us your money." It was hardly the kind of appeal that moved anyone present to flip open his checkbook.

How much such a failure of communication between the two groups can be ascribed to the shortcomings of the businessman is hard to say. On their part, many educators seem surprisingly ignorant of business purposes and practices—a result, no doubt, of their own devotion to their own specialties. But if the young executives were more hospitable toward the liberal arts, progress toward understanding between the business and the academic worlds would surely be easier. The emission from the young executives of a few simple signals indicating that they subscribed to the underlying objectives of learning in the humanities would help a great deal. And they need not read Keats to send out such signals, although it would not hurt if they did. Nor need they, as the young teacher suggested, "give us your profits"—even if they could. But of course some knowledge about what the underlying objectives are would have to precede the transmission of the signals.

The young executive could start on the acquisition of that knowledge in many ways. He might begin by taking a closer look at freedom and its meaning. The young executive—and in this respect he resembles his ancestors perhaps too much—has a fierce and concentrated affection for freedom in his own business. He wants freedom from government interference with the conduct of his business; he wants job mobility for himself; he wants all the freedom he needs in the choice of plant locations, in the transportation of goods; and he wants to be free to set his prices restricted as little as possible by the law, believing that the healthiest and most enduring and indeed the only sensible restriction will come from the marketplace. Freedom in all the exercises of a business operation, in short, he opts for and struggles for. But the central freedoms that underlie those other kinds he rarely speaks of or gives evidence of caring about. He is curiously blind to the relationship of his business freedom to the other freedoms, some of them of prime importance.

Addressing himself to this question, Columbia's Sidney Hook has pointed out that the problems of "bread and freedom" are very complicated, and that there is a tendency to blur the complication with "too easy identification of freedom with free enterprise. . . . Everyone who is wise about the conditions under which he enjoys his own freedom must be profoundly concerned about the state of freedom of the press and assembly, freedom of inquiry and teaching, freedom of cultural opportunity . . . intelligent moral choice depends on them. Business has seldom given any indication that it is aware of those strategic freedoms. There has been a tendency to ignore them except when a direct relationship of a most immediate kind with the narrow group interest could be demonstrated—like churches which spring into action with indignant protests when their communicants are interfered with in the freedom of worship, but which are strangely quiescent when the freedoms of other religious groups are violated. [The businessman] does not understand that freedoms are morally indivisible, [and he is not] concerned with the heritage of freedom. Although many businessmen are concerned with threats to free enterprise—especially when the threat takes the shape of government control in a rising economy—they have not displayed anywhere near the same zeal about improving the state of political freedom in their communities. They have contented themselves largely with renewed affirmations of faith in free enterprise . . . as if this constituted the alpha and the omega of the American faith in freedom."

Hook wrote those words some years ago, and he was talking about a different group of men from the young executives. And at least in the general statements and speeches made by the top officers of the business community, some increasing mention of the "strategic freedoms" seems to have been made in the last few years. But mention is not the same as action. With very few exceptions—and those usually occurred only when great pressure was either brought to bear or anticipated—the record of business has been dismal both on the issues of racial integration and on the question of anti-Semitism. The business community still seems to dwell largely in the Stone Age on those issues, almost never acting to encourage a swing away from anti-Negro and anti-Semite attitudes. Even some of the best-run companies, like Sears Roebuck, du Pont, and others, have conspicuously failed to lead any kind of social progress on such basic issues.

The young executive, of course, does not make his company's policy on these broad matters. But there is reason to think that he would not take a very enlightened view if he were involved. Racial, cultural, and political freedoms engage his interest very seldom. He does not seem any more enlightened than the older generation on the questions. He rarely feels called upon to speak out in behalf of freedom. One is nudged toward the conclusion that the young executive has very little understanding about the indivisibility of freedom, or, if he does understand it, he dismisses it as remote. He never seems to have been educated to understand it, and now he hasn't the time or the interest to obtain that education.

In the last couple of years, business managers have been laying a good deal of stress on their interest in "the generalist." They have been talking about the "well-rounded man," whom, so they say, they are always looking for. They stress the importance of having such men in the upper levels of management. "We have come to the conclusion," said one business member at a recent round-table discussion at Columbia University, "that exposure to a liberal arts education is the best possible preparation for meeting the future specialized demands of business." The statement has had plenty of recent echoes.

But its ring is not convincing. Sometimes, the expression of desire to employ liberal arts men seems to be riveted in—one can almost see the hand of the public relations man—after a long and more meaningful list of the kinds of qualifications that personnel directors really look for. "More than ever," Jack Rathbone of Jersey Standard wrote in his company's publication, *The Lamp,* "the oilman of the future will be highly trained. . . . About a quarter of Jersey Standard's professional, managerial and technical employees are chemical engineers. Another 20 per cent are trained in other engineering disciplines. Another 15 per cent are geologists, geophysicists, physicists, and mathematicians. . . . Business needs first-class administrators, economists, and—not the least important—thoughtful students of the historical and cultural environment in which modern business operates." It is hard to escape the view that the addition is indeed "least important."

A glance at any newspaper strengthens the belief. In demand by Esso are the specialists, like "polymer research chemist, solid propellant specialist, fiber development engineer, injection molding tech service engineer," and so on. Also needed are a "rheologist—resins" and a "rubber dynamicist," the former to study "relationships of resin parameters to end-use performance, investigating rheological behavior and evaluating alternative prediction techniques." Allis Chalmers wants "experienced fuel cell engineers and scientists," and

Pratt & Whitney has openings in "analog simulation" and "stress analysis/vibration." One looks in vain for the advertisement of an opening for the liberal arts graduate. If there is an opening for him, it usually comes after he has followed the liberal arts degree with a degree in business administration or some other kind of vocational training.

Of course the big companies admit that they are looking for the engineer, the chemist, the physicist, and the accountant. But the companies point out that while such men are essential to the gut operation of a business, top managers might come from more broadly educated groups. The fact is, however, as Mabel Newcomer wrote in *The Big Business Executive,* "the corporations themselves recruit primarily from graduates in engineering and business administration, and then select their executives from within. If graduate schools in business administration accept only graduates in science and engineering, then there is little chance that a man interested in a business career will select a liberal arts course, or that a corporation in search of a president will find many liberal arts graduates among its vice-presidents." Thus the actual practice of hiring that many companies now appear to be following is hardly calculated to encourage the liberal arts man in the hope that he can reach the top.

In the future the young executive may feel the lack of a liberal arts education. When his responsibilities broaden, he may be called on to deal with large questions—the broad relationships between the business community and the government, or between that community and the social currents running in the country. In those increasingly complex and increasingly important questions—which, like other aspects of American life, are subject to the accelerated process of change—the young executive is likely to prove no more competent than his predecessors. He is no better prepared for them than they were. He is no better gaited than they to cope with such matters. Thus the young executive has his deficiencies.

But the deficiency for which he has been most criticized obtains no longer: he is no cog in a machine, and it is fortunate for the summed-up good of U.S. industry that he is not. Through the dual and related processes of dissent and decision, the young executive has found in the corporate milieu an expression of his true individuality. Predominant in his shifting and ephemeral relationships with his company is his conviction that he can express himself as a free man through the organization, no matter how heavy its procedures and its protocol may weigh. Although they do not articulate their views in such philosophical terms, the young executives believe that they can live in a complex and demanding environment and still be free men. In characteristically concrete ways, they are demonstrating the truth of that conviction.

Listen to Them Talk

Education, culture, the arts—these are far out on the periphery of the young executive's vision. As issues, they interest him very little; as business problems, they come up very seldom. Yet snippets of opinion may surface.

Of Elvis Presley and Wolfgang Amadeus Mozart: *"Just because we release Elvis Presley records doesn't mean we're debasing American culture. We sell Mozart too, and we're just as anxious to do it. We lay it all out there, and we let the people take their choice. I've got no feeling that we are doing anything undesirable or wrong."*

Of doctorates and drivel, from a Ph.D.: *"I work about an hour and a half at home every night. Oh, my wife says it's really about three hours. But she doesn't make the same distinctions between work and other things that I do. Since I like economics, inevitably all of my reading is associated with my business. The* Survey of Current Business, Fortune, *the* Harvard Business Review, *parts of* Harper's . . . *that's one reason I enjoy my job, I enjoy the reading, I'm interested. My wife thinks I'm crazy, she likes to watch television. I watch TV maybe one hour a week. This drivel they write about the businessman not reading books . . . I have lots of friends who are quite literate. They read all the time, and they own the books.*

"Early in my career I missed out on a job with A.T.&T. because my competitor had a Ph.D. and I didn't. Probably on account of that, I decided to go ahead and get a Ph.D. Another reason was that I came from a family that was poorly

*educated but always had a high regard for education. My fa-
ther only finished the fourth grade in grammar school . . .
the way I looked at education, after the war the government
was willing to pay for it, all I had to do was put in the time.
Businessmen don't look down at the Ph.D., most will look up
at it. But in and of itself it will buy you nothing. A friend of
mine—and I know he'd like to have a Ph.D. really—says,
'It's a good thing you got that degree after you had a job. If
you had gotten the degree first, you never could have landed
the job at all.' "*

Of arms that scale and lights that fail, from a television
executive in charge of selling his network's programs: *"We
have the responsibility of the licensee in a federally regulated
business. Any buying of time has to be subject to our approval. We have at least as big a stake as any advertiser . . .
we have to concern ourselves with the total structure of the
programs, keeping diversity and balance. We've got a lot of
aggressive salesmen, and they've got to be kept in harmony,
and unleashed against the right targets—"*

*At this point he is interrupted by a phone call. He speaks to
the caller.* "What's that, Ed? A sponsor for that news program? Who is it?" *Pause.* "Oh, Stone Drug? What products?"
Pause. "A mouthwash, a tooth powder, a denture holder, and
a liquid that cures scaly arms? But we can probably knock the
scaly arm cure off the commercials?" *Pause.* "I'll call you."

*He phones his boss, listens. Then he talks once more to the
first caller.* "Ed, cooler heads have prevailed. Jack decided
against it. He thinks it would be unseemly. Those products—
well, one might have been okay but so many of them. And five
or six minutes . . . we can't do it." *He hangs up, turns away
from the phone.*

"In a way I'm torn. We need a sponsor. If we could have
gotten them to limit the number of products to two and only
mention them at the beginning and the end . . . if I thought
that could be done I'd argue with the boss. But I know the
prospective sponsors—they just wouldn't go for any such limitation."

Of soap and the Harvard Yard—from an advertising man in
a big agency: *"I really don't give a goddamn about soap. With
all the political and intellectual challenges of this job, and this
comfortable chair—and that's fairly important—one is still
pretty much a plumber. This job is nothing to be despised—*

but on the other hand, I consider myself something of an intellectual. I've read a lot; I've graduated from Harvard, and done graduate work. I've got a good liberal education; and the trouble is that I never feel I'm doing anything of intrinsic value. The alternatives have to do with a degree of excellence in the arts and sciences, or in political administration, and these do have a higher intrinsic value than advertising. I don't despise what I'm doing, but I do say there's a distinction. I think with all this reading, and Harvard and that stuff, wouldn't it be great if I could write a book or something. So I think from time to time that I'm a failure. This bugs me."

Chapter FOUR

The Man and the Corporation

The group we have defined as "the young executives" contains a high proportion of strong-minded and strongly motivated individuals. They are highly effective *ad hoc* operators with a factual turn of mind, a penchant for pragmatism, and little interest in the humanistic disciplines. Possessing both technical competence and exasperating self-confidence, today's young executives are in turn possessed—by a consuming drive for more and more promotions in the business world. They are perpetually pushing for more personal responsibility and more personal freedom in their business activities—forever searching for the formula which will bring them that freedom of action in the big-company environment. They are certain that they can stay in the organization, progress through it, perhaps one day assume command of it—and all the while serve their inner standards, all the while satisfy the howling man within.

Their loyalty they keep largely for themselves. But they are able to do this and still give a very large segment of themselves to their company. They work hard—so hard that, with only token resistance from them, business preoccupations penetrate into the furthermost corners of their lives. They devote their considerable education and business experience to furthering the interests of their company. While they are in a company's employ, they assent to its fundamental purposes and its objectives. That assent, however, is far different from the dependence and the submission that in the past have been popularized as typical. The terrible temper of these men—their angry kind of confidence, their relentless insistence on their own capaci-

66

ties, their unremitting shove toward achievement—makes subservience impossible. Responding to that terrible temper, the organization—because of its recognition of what these men can do—is endeavoring to accommodate these perennial attackers, and to create a new kind of atmosphere of tension that will encourage them. It is this new atmosphere that coaxes the man to give a great deal of himself to the organization.

In return for that segment of themselves that they give, the young executives demand a lot. Their allegiance to their company is curious, complex, and conditional. Under some circumstances they are quick to withdraw it. When they are disappointed in their expectations of the way they should be rewarded—with money and, more important to them, with "more challenge and more responsibility"—they terminate their relations with their company quickly and finally. When they find themselves unable to change a policy that affects them and that they disapprove of, they often leave for greener pastures. Or in still another complicated but frequent response, they may find themselves at a middle level of dissent: they may continue to render their loyalty on fundamentals, but at the same time devote themselves to bucking old organizational procedures and to fighting old organizational ideas in order to plant an innovation that they believe to be desirable. They are willing to see the corporate trophies that they covet, and compete so fiercely for, awarded or withheld in accordance with the success of the innovation they introduce.

In their drive for those rewards may lie the seeds of future defeat for some of these men. For they are enlisted in, and heavily committed to, the service of "the Bitch Goddess, Success." In her modern corporate embodiment, the Bitch Goddess' attributes are quite different from the ones ascribed to her in other times: she is not an idol appeased only by gold, and she cannot be served without regard to standards of decency and morality. But in one respect she is unchanged: she has maintained her capacity to thwart men. Every capable manager, every young executive, cannot win the ultimate responsibility, the position of chief executive. Someday, many young executives, by then not so young, will have to take down the sails of their ambition. They will face some hard adjustments, especially in view of the narrow range of their cultural activities. Of those who do not make it to the top, some will be able to bank their competitive fires, and sustain their interest in business—an interest that by then will have a large field for expression—even when they know that they can climb up no longer. Others, however, may end their careers in disappointment and defeat—even for some of its abler members these are inevitable attendants in a society organized upon competition.

But for the present, defeat could not be further from the young executive's mind. He is strongly motivated, experienced, and at the height of his powers. At his level of management— different, perhaps, than at the top, where the swirl of great events may make some problems forever resistant to the application of intelligence—everything before him seems to admit of a solution. All he wants is world enough, and time—and elbowroom. With them—or so it seems to him—he can make any problem that comes along bend to his strong practical will.

And the organization is flexing to adapt to him. As the business world becomes more fluid, more open to innovation, corporations demand executives who have a high degree of initiative and self-reliance. The presence of such men in management—with their keenness for advancement, their demand for personal responsibility, and their insistence that every step forward carry with it the promise of yet another step beyond— speeds up the changes that are occurring in the business organization itself. This parallel shift in the character of the men and the nature of the organizations is in an early phase.

Like successful men, successful companies live in danger of putting on fat. They can become immobile, unresponsive, inflexible, and empty, long before those disabilities show up in the numbers columns. They can suppress argument, unmindful of the admonition of John Stuart Mill that "all silencing of discussion is an assumption of infallibility." Those are dangers that began with the beginning of organization—with that fabled moment when two men came together to move a stone.

But a company cannot prevent adding years, and it can hardly deny itself some normal growth. Further, it cannot deny itself success, even though sometimes success—especially when it comes from the ability to carry out a single activity extremely well—may be a bad preparation for the many other activities that change may introduce. As a result, a big and successful company inclines to become slow in its reactions, stiff in its resistances, and demanding in its protocol. None are able to ward off all the bureaucratic rigidities, all the tedious forms and formalities. Inefficiencies creep in, and incompetent people dig in. Manuals of procedure, and the people who defend them, have a disposition to grow thicker every year. The protocol that attends the visit of company brass can be as encumbering as the trappings that surround the visit of a chief of state.

Yet alert companies manage to avoid fatal disease by constant adjustment to changing reality. The process is similar to the one that John Gardner in *Self Renewal* prescribes for social organizations, an ecological development he likens to "a total garden . . . [where] some things are being born, other things are flourishing, still other things are dying—but the system lives on." Pond life is as good an analogy as the total garden. When such a balanced process is maintained, the company can stay healthy. The fact that it is born does not mean that it must die.

Essential to the maintenance of that kind of organic health is what Gardner calls "a framework of expectation." The organization must recognize its own vital need for innovation— for the process that in the new business lexicon is being called "creative activity"—and it must see that such activity is encouraged and not stifled by its own bureaucratic weight. Some companies have already become conscious and explicit about their responsibilities in this regard. David Sarnoff of R.C.A. declared recently, "We like experimentation here. An air of inquiry, a welcome for novelty and change, those are the attitudes we try to encourage." I.B.M., G.E., and others are just as aware of the importance of a policy like that.

Other companies maintain an atmosphere congenial to growth without consciously articulating a philosophy. Kaiser Industries—the complex of companies that includes Kaiser Aluminum, Kaiser Steel, Kaiser Jeep, as well as cement, engineering, and construction companies—keeps itself fresh and refurbished in an effortless way. Lots of cool clean air blows through the organization because of the personality of Edgar Kaiser, a man who views himself with the critical eye of a perfectionist, who wants to hear the reasons why he may be wrong—and who is accepted through the company, by those who disagree with some of his policies as well as by those who agree with him, as a special kind of leader. The Gillette Company and others have their own ways of keeping the organization air-conditioned.

Some companies are not yet cognizant of the importance of "the framework of expectation." The American Can Company has had lots of trouble giving to its young executives the responsibilities are the latitude for action that they want. Public utilities, banks, and railroads, with numerous exceptions, have some of the same kind of trouble—partly because of the nature of their business, partly because some of their chief executives haven't looked around keenly enough. But change is coming to them, too.

While he works for any given company, the young executive finds much that he can agree with. Implicit in his striving for "more challenge and more responsibility" is his acceptance of the organization's criteria of success. The two standards of value—the man's and the organization's—usually coincide. From that coincidence comes a kind of harmony, a sense of sharing. The man does not fight a war of principles against his surroundings. He agrees that the organization should exist, that it should survive, that it should grow and make a profit. In such basic areas where the organization, like the modern state, insists on the consent of its citizens, the man can grant it without any sacrifice of conscience or compromise with moral precept. Both man and organization accept the fact that, reverting to the ecological analogue, to put a shark in the pond would be to end all forms of life there. And, since their goals correspond, the young executive wants to see the organization not dead but flourishing.

Another tacit but basic assent is the one that the young executive pays to the need for organization in the modern business world. In coming to this view, these men are conditioned by their pasts. If there really ever was a simpler epoch of rugged individualism, when the two-fisted businessman hunted down business problems the same way he hunted bears —by crashing through the brush, leveling his rifle, and firing —the young executives never lived in it. They never knew the frustrations that the former generation encountered as the problems became more subtle and persistent, the bear harder to identify, and whether or not to pull the trigger a matter for committee discussion. The organization never sprang up around these men, to web them in or constrain them. Instead, it has always been there—the *sine qua non* of any attempt to solve intricate and pluralistic business problems, the kind that the young executives these days are forever struggling with. As a result, the young executives, in a realistic appraisal, regard the organization as an essential expression of business life: they lend their unspoken consent to the comment of John Gardner that "complexity seems to be the universal condition, and organization the universal requirement."

To William H. Whyte, Jr., in *The Organization Man,* these

provisions of the tacit pact between man and organization meant a denial "that there is—or should be—a conflict between individual and organization. The denial is bad for the organization. It is worse for the individual. What it does, in soothing him, is to rob him of the intellectual armor that he so badly needs . . . In seeking an ethic that offers a spurious peace of mind, thus does he tyrannize himself." Now, however, the vital importance of the conflict between man and organization is emerging—at different speeds, and to different degrees, depending on the organization—into a tacit understanding on the part of both groups. Unlike the organization man, the young executive does not strive for a spurious peace of mind. He is made of different metal.

The agreements between modern man and modern organization are not like the laws of the Medes and the Persians. They were not made to stand forever. They are constituted of general affinities, not hardened bonds. The two poles—man and organization—are constantly changing, and the magnetic field that lies between them changes, too. The man periodically examines his own attitude toward the organization, and gauges its attitude toward him. If he doesn't like what he sees, he tries to change it. If he can't change it, he moves.

The man's own value in the marketplace enters at this point. "I think we all recognize that we have something there is a market for," coolly says one young executive on behalf of his generation, and he is quite right. These men are in short supply. And they are at an age, according to one study, of "intense self-assessment"—measuring where they stand today against some internal, self-drawn, and very important calendar of progress. They are not yet ready, as they may be ten to fifteen years from now, to restrict their own advancement in return for retirement benefits and pension plans. They are still mobile.

Fortune's sampling of their ranks showed that three out of five of these men have worked for more than one company; of the more-than-one-company group, one out of four has worked for three to five different companies. "If I were asked to get people who wouldn't leave, I could do it," says Dr. Frank McCabe, director of executive personnel for I.T.T. "It would be easy. But you might not have any company left after a while. The more successful you are in attracting the comers, the higher your potential turnover rate is. The comers are movers. If they can't move on to more responsible positions inside, they'll go to another company. Their loyalty depends

upon the company's willingness to provide challenges and rewards in the job situation. After they have gotten on top of a
particular job, they feel that, as far as debt to the company
goes, on any given day everybody's even." Caspar Ordal, director of management development and recruitment for
Colgate-Palmolive, adds, "We've got to create opportunities
for this man to take responsibilities when he's ready—that's
extremely important." And the man himself vigorously agrees.

He agrees so much, in fact, that departure day can come
very soon after he ascertains that his attitude toward the
proper timing of rewards differs from the company's. In an
illustrative case, W. R. Grace & Co. judged a few years ago
that one of its bright young men was not yet ready for a vice-
presidential job. The company gave the job to an older out-
sider, and tried to assuage the younger man's feelings by coun-
seling patience and holding out the promise of salary increases. But the young man wanted, more than anything else,
the prize of the bigger job, which held, of course, "more challenge and more responsibility." The counsel of patience he
chose to ignore. "My feeling was," this executive recently recalled, "that if they didn't think I was qualified then, they
might feel the same way three to five years later. I guess I
assumed that at some point in time the job would be mine. But
I wasn't sure that I would enjoy the interim." He resigned.
"This kind of thing is inevitable sometimes," says a personnel
man. "When you deal with people with a great deal of drive,
you know there are some situations they're not sufficiently patient to sit out."

The same thing can happen when views of the organization's purposes diverge. The organization may move off in a
policy direction that the man disapproves of; after a period of
time he may conclude he never can share in this new purpose;
then man and company are soon parted. A financial executive
left a company headquartered in Chicago some time ago because in his judgment the company was putting far too much
emphasis on high foreign earnings. "The markets where the
company raised its capital were unrelated to the geographical
areas where earnings were derived," he says. "I tried to push
the company into a staid but steady business in the U.S. But
top management kept thinking of it as a glamour company—
they were very stock-market-minded. I felt the whole thing
had to come to a screeching halt. I didn't want to be associated
with that, so I left."

To leave the organization is the ultimate dissent. But every day of his life the young executive is carrying on a whole range of lesser dissents that stop short of the ultimate one. These lesser dissents, these bits of innovative thought and process, generate the tension that constitutes a vital force in the life of the organization, and its greatest guarantee that it will not be left in the backwash of change. Many companies are already taking cognizance of the salient importance of the tension born of innovation. "We're looking for individuals who are innovative," says Ordal. Another executive says, "The word 'team' isn't very popular around here." The president of U. S. Freight, Morris Forgash, notes, "You can't get results from a guy who agrees with his boss. That's like having a meeting with yourself. In an interview I had with a man recently, I tried to provoke him into a little yessing. When he didn't go for it, I hired him." Herbert Schoeck, until lately officer in charge of executive development for Jersey Standard, says, "We want people who like to spread their wings a bit."

Igniting these innovative processes are the young executives. They are men who know the techniques required to change the organization, who know how to put their shoulders to the organizational wheels and make the organization move, how to bend the organization to their will. According to myths about these men, when they elected to work for a big company they disappeared into the Gray Immensity—they sank back, with a sigh, into the enveloping arms of a great corporation. They sank into the yogurt-like blandness that Whyte called the imprisonment of brotherhood. But for the able young man in a big company today, there is no imprisonment of brotherhood.

To impel the organization to innovate involves qualities that are quite the opposite of conformity. The process required to plant a change in corporate ground calls for stubborn conviction and dogged application, as well as a disregard for minor frictions and frustrations. "Sure, I get frustrated around here," is a universal cry. But in order to accomplish his objective the man will put up with the frustration: characteristically, the young executive puts his emphasis on being effective.

In the service of that cause he finds dispassionate persistence a highly useful quality. One man spent a good deal of time for a year and a half working up a proposal, and when he made it to the board, "they clobbered me." But he says, "The problem was one of timing. I'm going to try again. I noticed one man on the board who wasn't against it—he was neutral, and he said later that there was one area that had not been explained. I have a man right now getting figures on that area."

Another young executive is pushing for a sweeping organizational change in one of the nation's biggest companies. He is troubled by the fact that many in his company do not share his sense of urgency about the reorganization. He says that his bosses "admit that the present system is wrong, but they say this isn't the time to change it. But I'm uneasy with things the way they are. I think our future success demands this change. I've been plugging away at this for a year. I haven't set any ultimatum time—I don't think in those terms. But we've had some changes in top management, and I'm going at it harder than ever this year."

A man who works for a big life-insurance company—and who has moved up in the organization at a rate far faster than is usual in that business—admits that he often runs into committees who debate and water down some of his objectives. "But that doesn't cause me to change what I want," he says. "I just keep working on it, selling, persuading, motivating, convincing. Ultimately, I'll get it. The problem doesn't shake me up at all—it's part of the challenge."

Behind such constraint lies the young executive's desire for accomplishment. He suppresses the emotional part of himself in order to permit the more developed part—the part that is gratified by accomplishment—to succeed. What has been mislabeled compliance is thus, in a psychological sense, maturity. "I find I suppress a little bit of myself all the time," confesses an aggressive young man who works for a big oil company. "Otherwise, I'd be too rebellious—I'm told that I have been, sometimes. A little rebellion is a good thing, but if you don't tone it down, and pick your spots, you accomplish nothing. There's no point in swimming upstream with your mouth open. It's better to make a 10 percent change than no change."

The young executive is not swept with remorse if he loses an occasional argument. To be victimized by self-blame when he fails to win his company superiors over to his own way of thinking would be to defeat his own purposes. "When I first came here," says one man, "I felt a personal sense of failure when I was convinced I was right and I got overruled. I've since learned that there is no point in this, it doesn't get you anyplace. Sometimes I wake up at night and think that if I had put it a different way, I would have gotten it. But really all I can do is bring in all my arguments, to the point where they say, 'We've heard all your arguments, now here's the decision.'

When I lose, I try to find out why—to learn something that may help next time."

Another man puts the matter differently. He is perhaps given to more introspection than most of his peers, and his analysis points up the dual nature of the young executive's life in a big corporation—the urge for expression on the one hand, the need for constraint on the other. "You have to have enough emotional response—enough burn—to keep you driving ahead," he says. "If you have none of that burn, the first time somebody comes up to you and says, 'You can't do this, it won't work,' you'll agree and give up. So you need the burn. But you have to learn to control it—you must not be emotional in your responses when somebody criticizes you."

Another manager recalls the time when his company sent him to work under a much older man. He found the department in a state of considerable disorder. But, with an eye toward the attainable, he began the process of revamping it with caution. "The control functions were out of line, the services and general atmosphere were not what they should have been," he recalls. "That was the reason for my going there in the first place. But the No. 1 man was about to retire, and he was skeptical about a lot of things. You had to face the facts of the situation. Here was this individual who had been with that organization for forty-five years. He operated more like the father of a family than a businessman. His major concern was for the welfare of individuals rather than the business—and you can get into all sorts of social arguments about the merits of that. His people were doing a job—of sorts. But in that area of people, this man was incapable of permitting change. Going into a situation like that, you don't dare to make a false step. You may have to spend three years correcting a bad impression. I spent the time before he retired identifying the problems, lining things up in logical order, sequencing. There were some of his pet areas that I didn't even attempt to include. There was no point in it at that time. They were things we had to put off until later on, after he had retired."

Listen to Them Talk

How aware is the young executive of the expectant atmosphere in the organization he works for? How much is that atmosphere worth to him?

"I like what I'm doing. We always have some interesting project going on. Recently another company, in insurance, offered me a big increase and some appealing blocks of stock options. I turned it down—I've got enough to live on, and I'll get more. The trouble with the insurance company offer—they wanted me to go in as second man, to succeed the president someday. The president himself said to me, 'I'll keep my seat warm for you, the people around me are the palace guard.' But what kind of a guy is it who after fifty years on the job hasn't got anyone around him to take his place? And what kind of an organization is that? Oh, it offered me a big jump in income—from $20,000 to $65,000, and the prospect of being president. But I had already broken through to the point where all my bills were being paid. I decided to stay where I was."

Another man, in a totally different business context, has a roughly similar reaction:

"We've had this internal disagreement about how to push a new product. Right now it looks like the way I favored won't win out. I'm not sure who's right and who's wrong—it will depend on how the product goes. If the product is successful —well, I'll be convinced I was wrong. If it is sort of successful, I'll think 'Well, that's the odds.' If it fails, I'll figure they would have done better my way.

"I'll say I told you so, sure. But you try not to be too much of a pain in the neck saying that after it's all over. And I won't end up feeling 'this goddamn organization.' I did at the place I worked before this. I just quit one day. I was fed up, and I walked out. Here, it's a pleasant day-to-day situation. There's hardly any pressure for conformity and such stuff. Of course,

the company has a boss—it isn't a democracy. Once the boss makes a decision you're not supposed to work at cross purposes with him. In this sense, I suppose you could say there's not toleration of dissent. But up to the point where he says, 'This is what we're going to do,' there's tremendous toleration. And there's no grudge held against the dissenter. Nor does the guy who loses out to another guy's point of view hold a grudge against the winner. Not usually, anyway. It would depend a little on how arbitrary the other fellow was, and how the decision he insisted on came out. If he were very determined, and it turned out badly, I'd be a little sore. After all, I'm a stockholder in this company, and if something turns out badly, I lose, and our prestige is hurt."

Chapter FIVE

The Man and His Decisions

The man sits at his desk. But what does he do there? If one could peer over his shoulder, and watch the flow of work across the desk, what kind of situations would one find the young executive dealing with? What kind of decisions does he make, what managerial qualities does he display? What are his pleasures and rewards? The situations are complicated, but fascinating; the managerial qualities are highly polished and professional; and the gratifications are vitally important—the more so because this is a man who lives his life essentially in one context, the context of his business.

His success over a decade or more of business life has brought him lots of business acreage to plow. In the longer view of the corporation, it is acreage that comes only temporarily under his care. Yet the young executive worries over its vigor, examines its changing state of health, and cultivates its present profitability and future promise much as he would if it were to be his own forever. But in return for the personal nature of that involvement, the young executive looks for freedom of managerial action. He is psychologically so constructed that he can maintain his own interest in and his own dedication to his job only if he has a commensurate opportunity to make his own decisions. Wide as the domains under his control may be, he is forever elbowing to make them wider still. He wants the latitude to decide, to innovate, and to make changes, and he wants that latitude continually to enlarge as he progresses. Indeed, he equates his progress with increases in his responsibility.

That much-desired individual responsibility the young executive finds in the context of a group environment. It seems to him perfectly natural that he should have a big company at his back. Its looming presence, to be sure, can curb and circumscribe: the corporation can be hard to move, it may be committee-ridden or as multilayered as French pastry. At times, the young executive believes the behemoth to be not so much at his back as on it: he groans with frustration over lengthy procedures he must occasionally follow and long stretches of time he must sometimes spend in committee meetings.

Yet the frustrations rarely become so acute that they cancel out the advantages that men like the young executives find in working for a big company. The whole purpose of their lives is to be effective. And the big corporation has resources, reservoirs of strength, which the young manager, if he is expert enough, can tap in such a manner that they extend his own effectiveness without jeopardizing his individual control. In that way his personal powers can be supported and enlarged through the faculty of the big organization. In a small company, the margin for experiment and innovation is likely to be thin. New endeavors probably cannot be sustained for very long. And small companies may tend to concentrate important decisions at one key point in the organization—the office of the boss.

But large organizations have the means to encourage and to sustain new undertakings. Not only in their physical laboratories, but in their managerial ones as well, they can afford to support what the young executive calls "creative activity." Further, because of the magnitude and diversity of their businesses, they usually decentralize, delegating wide fields of action to their divisional and departmental managers. That means that many big companies have scattered and multiple points of responsibility within their ranks.

The thrust of decision comes from those points—from the upper and middle levels, more than from the top. Most decisions do not descend from the monarch, as they did in the splendid century; instead, they push up from below, for review and approval at the top. That puts the young executive precisely where he wants to be: at the crucial point of decision.

To stand on such crucial ground whets his desire for liberty of action. His bosses above him have final intramural authority, of course, but they are often concerned with matters which, in the end, they can only observe, comment about, and regard with hope. And the people on the rungs below the young executive may be mere witnesses to problems whose origin and resolution seem remote to them. But the young executive faces external situations that, while manifold and intricate, generally appear both to be susceptible of his solution, and proximate to his hand. Further, he has available the means precisely to measure the soundness of many of his decisions: their results are apt to show in cost reductions, production increases, or some other quantitative respect—just the kind of material improvement that is calculated to appeal to a pragmatist. And those improvements are highly visible to every corporate eye, thus bringing within the grasp of this success-minded man the cherished prize of recognition—the corporate and professional recognition of merit that a big company can grant him, and that he wants so badly.

Many of the profoundest pleasures of his business life, therefore, come to the young executive because he works for a big corporation. It is precisely the enhancement of difficulty, the intensification of intricacy that big companies lend to business situations that increase the satisfactions that this man takes in dealing with them. Hence his consuming—and, to his wife at least, his often tedious and extravagant—appetite for his business. Were it all easier, the young executive would like it all much less. In the current mythology about American business, the big corporation has been represented as smothering and mothering men. It may mother and smother those who are not so able as the young executives. But to the men who meet its criteria of competence, the big company is just as likely to give exactly what they want: the authority to deal with business situations that can be positively arabesque in their complexity.

How a young executive shows his independence and judgment in a demanding big-company environment is nowhere better illustrated than by the role he plays in situations which attend the acquisition and the spin-off of companies. The process of augmenting or diminishing the corporate structure by those means is a big-company process, but it leaves plenty of opportunity for individual initiative and action. The young executive carries out a good deal of the spadework that precedes the decision by top management to acquire or spin off; indeed, the initial impulse to take such a step may very well come from him. Or he may be the man who, after the acquisition has taken place, finds himself confronted with new business problems to solve—including the problem of establishing a whole new set of relationships with bosses and peers whom he knows very little about. In either case, the inclination of these modern young managers is not to search for a pattern to conform to—a search that would prove fruitless anyway—but to exert their abilities and exercise their judgments in accordance with their own estimate of what "the good of the business" demands. In the convoluted process of acquisition and spin-off, the young executive finds an important individual role to play.

In the illustrative cases that follow, fictitious names for both man and company have been used. All of the interviews in which this material was acquired were confidential. Interestingly enough, when many of the young executives were later approached with a request that the restrictions on the interviews be lifted, they seemed undisturbed by the thought, even though they had discussed their business affairs with surprising candor. But for the most part, the confidential lid was kept on by the company managements themselves, who exercised their option to withhold attribution.

The first case concerns Edward Jones, thirty-nine, a vice-president and a division chief for Tubes, Inc., a company which makes containers both for its own product lines and for outside sale. Jones came to Tubes, Inc., when it acquired a smaller company that he had worked for as a production engineer. In a manner typical of the young executives, Jones had worked hard and in a consciously planned direction since the beginning of his business career. "I started as a section personnel chief, and then became an assistant personnel manager," recalled Jones recently. "I was thirty years old, and I thought I was on top of the world. Then I decided that the only way to get ahead was to go into operations. I was a fair-haired boy, so I started in manufacturing as a supervisor. But I discovered that it was impossible to schedule production unless I knew the manufacturing operation better. So I worked from 8:30 A.M. to 5:00 P.M. on my job and then I worked the full second shift on the lines. I had three hours' sleep a night for nine months. Later, the president of our company wanted me for his assistant. I handled mostly sales. In six months I was general sales manager. I had research and product development under me, then I became vice-president of sales. Then I got this job."

After Tubes, Inc., acquired his company, Jones got his first big job for his new employer, which came as a result of still another acquisition. He was designated to consolidate what had become a Tubes, Inc., division with a newer acquisition, which also made containers. Jones remembers vividly his reaction when he first looked over the newly acquired plant at Easton, Pennsylvania. The Easton plant was losing substantial amounts of money at the time. Jones recalls: "At Easton they had four floors of an old factory. On the top floor they were extruding. Then they buggy-loaded down to the third floor, where they headed the tube, then down to the second floor for another operation. I took one look at the way it was being operated—and I knew we had to relocate. I figured we had one year to put it in the black. I knew we had to make money, or throw the key away.

"Easton had some 400 white-collar people. We chopped that down to fifty. We chucked equipment out of the door—literally, we dumped it into a pond nearby. Some of it was brand-new, but it had absolutely no value. We spent $4 million on the right kind of new equipment. We put all the operations on one floor. Everything was unitized and conveyorized. It was a pretty difficult period. But within a year production was turned around."

But the problems at Easton went beyond the production lines. Jones found that policies governing sales were either nonexistent or ill advised, and putting his own sales experience to work, he set about reshaping them. "The trouble was," Jones explains, "that at Easton they were always thinking of more sales—but as sales went up, profits went down. Salesmen would go out and sell anything, and then the plant had the problem of developing the equipment to make the product. The plant was behind on deliveries as much as a year. Manufacturing was shifting back and forth instead of finishing a run. Customers were so annoyed that they would call the chief executive, or any other officer at the parent company they could get to listen."

That was a situation which called for an assertion of local authority. "Right in the middle of the booming but unprofitable business we stopped half the production lines. We told the customers to go to blazes. We told our single biggest customer that if they didn't like it they'd have to find someone else. I was pretty sure they wouldn't cut us out. We advised our St. Louis headquarters to say they had no control over us whatever. We tried to be sympathetic to customers, but when we scheduled an order, we ran that order. The schedule couldn't be changed without my approval.

We established minimum orders and specific neck types and

colors. If someone wanted a different item, the order would have to be substantial, and the customer would have to pay the development costs. We were pretty hard-nosed about this. Salesmen said that if we didn't take the small orders we would lose the big orders. We said, 'We just can't do it.' I felt that if a salesman was worth his weight he could tell a customer to go to blazes in such a way that it wouldn't hurt the business. I honestly didn't care whether we lost customers or not. My job right then was to get us in the black. If we couldn't do it within a year I would have recommended that we get rid of the whole thing."

The series of fast decisions that this recasting required gave Jones no trouble at all. Assured and emphatic about his own powers in such situations, Jones says, "It's no problem for me to make a decision." His capacity to do just that is shown by the results of a quick side trip he made to another of the division's plants in Mexico. "I spent a week down there," says Jones, "and I decided we ought to sell the plant. I could see that we wouldn't be able to operate in the way that the situation required. The history was complicated, but it was obvious there was going to be too much hanky-panky for us. So we sold the plant off, and took a loss, and got out."

Jones' relations with Tubes, Inc., headquarters during this period were unique but illustrative. He had not been associated with the company for very long, and he had not yet established a very clear identity of interest with it. He says frankly today that "it was a real tough hassle then. They were trying to gobble us up. It looked as though our responsibility was going to be only manufacturing and sales. You can't operate that way. You need full scope." And, at the time, Jones was impatient with Tubes, Inc., procedures. Says he: "We threw their book of procedures out the window. We didn't have time to explain and justify everything to St. Louis—we just said the heck with it. They wanted us to fill out forms 800 and 801. You spent six months preparing the forms and six months getting them approved. By that time, it was too late. So on our own we spent $2 million, and we filled out the forms afterward. There was hell to pay at the time, but it worked. If it had gone sour, I would have been fired for sure.

"But our relations with Tubes, Inc., have improved tremendously since those early days. I have full responsibility now. And I submit forms, but they've zipped up the procedure— you submit a form, and if you hear nothing in two weeks you go ahead. Of course we owe Tubes, Inc., something—they had the bucks to give us what we wanted. Now we've arrived. It's obvious to me that this is going to be tremendous—potentially, our division has the most to offer Tubes, Inc., in products and profit. I'd love to have this business for my own right now."

In revamping and consolidating those business segments, Jones was working as what the business world calls "a generalist." The word has a special business meaning. Jones would not be considered a generalist in the judgment of the academic world: although a liberal arts graduate, he describes himself as "a man with a mechanical aptitude," and he wishes he had taken engineering instead. ("I'd like my son to take engineering. It's particularly helpful today.") But he is a business generalist, having business experience in several specialties, not just one. That may still leave him, in the view of academia, a man of limited intellectual horizons. But Jones hardly cares about that. Listen to him talk about what does interest him: "We're aggressively going after new developments. One big area that plastic tubing hasn't touched yet has been dentifrice tubes. Because of the oils, everyone has always used metals. But metal tubes are very competitive. There are fifteen companies that make them now, there isn't much profit any more. It's an overhead carrier. Our objective is to obsolete the metal tube business. We've developed a ten-layer laminated tube of plastic and metal, plastic inside and outside, metal in between to hold the oils. The fluoride won't react on the plastic. Our equipment for making the tube runs at eighty a minute, but at a new plant we have a program to get it up to 260 a minute. It's a good profit item, and we've started selling the tube to a huge toothpaste manufacturer. Right now we have 60 percent of the business for this tube, but that won't last. Still, when the real competition comes along, they'll have to start by making eighty a minute."

Wrapped up in business though he is, Jones occasionally pauses to regard the man within. In a revelatory dialogue, he finds himself content—restless to work, but content with his assertive, confident, pragmatic self, whose needs are met and whose appetites are slaked by progress in the external world, an Aristotelian world of many thoughts and many processes. "Am I satisfied? I'm an egotist, and anything that works out well is just fine. I've turned down other offers. I don't think I've made a mistake. Even at triple the salary, I don't want people looking over my shoulder. I don't like the idea of reporting to people every move I make. The autonomy that Tubes, Inc., has given us is a vote of confidence. They've given me this opportunity. I don't feel pushed off in a corner. I hope my accomplishments will speak for themselves when I move up later on.

"But I'm not going to follow the party line if my judgment tells me I should be doing something else. I don't like flattery, people telling me I'm doing a good job. I want people to tell me my shortcomings. And I don't want a lot of yes men around me. I want guys to speak up. Then, once the matter has been fully discussed, I'll say, 'I've made a decision' and that's it. No backbiting, no little cliques. There's a lot of pressure on me, and I try to keep the pressure on the guys who work for me. I'm in early and I work late—and I want them in early, and I want them to work late. I want the fellows who work for me to be after my job."

The view that congenial social relationships, or the maintenance of heavy joviality at office parties, are important ingredients in business success is contravened by Jones' experience. He rarely sees his superiors after business hours, or for any purpose except the explicit conduct of business affairs. And he just as rarely socializes with his subordinates. "I remain aloof on a social basis. I don't want to know their personal problems. I can be a soft touch on occasion. Somebody started to tell me that my secretary was getting a divorce, but I interrupted right away. I just don't want to know that kind of thing."

Coming to the end of his dialogue, Jones notes with satisfaction his immersion in his work. "I never resent the amount of time I spend on my job," he says. "Maybe I can't be a very good father to my children. I don't see enough of them on this kind of schedule. But I don't expect my work to diminish. I enjoy it. I find it very difficult to relax. I just don't like time on my hands. I'd be bored stiff with too much time off."

In another situation, an acquisition by a big company also spiced a young executive's business life. But in this case the young man was important in the decision to acquire, and then went on to assume the responsibility for polishing up the new possession of the parent company afterward. Where the previous problem called primarily for forcefulness of decision—a single-minded drive to a clear objective—here the managerial requirements were very different: needed was a velvet glove, or perhaps a pair of them. In this case, the young executive, whom we shall call Tom, is chief accountant for a southern company whose sales this year will run around $150 million. His company acquired last year a $7-million company in the

Midwest, with products quite unrelated to its own. The man who founded, built up, and headed the smaller company for twenty-five years before the acquisition has been retained, by a decision of the top management of the purchasing company, as president of what now has become a division. For three years before the purchase the performance of the small company was lackluster; Tom is now seeking to polish it.

He got the responsibility for the new division, which he now carries in addition to his work as chief accountant, by the simple expedient of asking for it. "Ordinarily, one waits for a responsibility like that to be assigned," Tom says. "You usually don't volunteer, because management is often already aware of the problem and has decided how to solve it. But I always wanted an operational job, and as an accountant I was closely involved with this acquisition in the first place. So in this case I broke one of the cardinal rules. I spoke to George about involving myself in the new management. I knew he didn't have time for it, and I did. And I guess my timing was right."

After he had the job, Tom quickly discovered where the delicacy of its performance lay: in the management of relationships with the founder of the smaller company. The young executive could not barge in and make changes so drastic that the older man, for so long prince of his own satrapy, would find them intolerable. Yet many operational changes had to be made if the division's performance was to measure up to the higher standards of the company that acquired it. "The first problem is the president," Tom observes. "I could shatter him, but I won't. For now, I'm a hero-maker. I'm going to change him from a $7-million-company president to a $40-million one. He used to think about $100,000 for research, and now I'm telling him about $1,500,000—he isn't used to figures like that, he doesn't understand them. I'm going to show him how —but I'm dealing with a strong personality, a man twenty years older than I am. My biggest problem is teaching him how to think about his problems—to think bigger, now that he's got us behind him, but not to come to conclusions so quickly." Then comes the note of personal obligation, tacitly understood: "I have accepted the fact, although nobody actually told me, that the results of his conclusions will be my responsibility. Once we have our target set up, it's up to me— so things are going to stay on the track."

To keep things on the track, however, required a special kind of diplomacy. "One big problem," says Tom, "is the way the president liked to make intuitive judgments instead of studying the situation. I had to shut down his office in Los Angeles. He said, 'Tom, I don't want to close the Los Angeles office.' I said, 'But let's study what would happen if we did.' We had a study made, the savings were five times what he thought they were. We're shutting down. Then he wanted to open a small plant in Philadelphia. I have accounting make a study of the cost of opening a plant in Philadelphia, versus the cost of air freight, the cost of deferred air freight, the cost of rail shipment, et cetera. As soon as I show him, the plant goes out the window and we're on deferred air freight."

The remaking of a president and the making of products blended in this situation. The young executive had a two-headed problem to solve: the products had to be changed, but it was someone else whom he had to instill with the desire to change them. "This is one of the few companies making its kind of components that makes both a product for itself, and a private label," explains Tom. "That private label product, made under a contract, was a pretty big part of the business. It was looked on as profitable, because you don't have any marketing expense. But it turned out the product was hard to make, especially with the equipment the company had. The president was fascinated with it, devoted a lot of time to it, but couldn't make it successful. Morale was suffering, and so were the other lines. I let it run for two months. I could see the president's anger at the people who couldn't solve it. Then I brought in electronics engineers, I proved it was a very sophisticated product. They were lucky to be making it as well as they were." Again a pragmatic note: "The drive to succeed wasn't realistic. But when I mentioned discontinuing the private-label product, the president kept worrying about the payroll. I told him with our resources he didn't have to worry, that we'd take care of meeting the payroll. What he had to do was think objectively about this product. I finally got the president's head turned around, and we canceled the private-label contract."

Just as he brought in electronics engineers to analyze the difficulties on the production line, so the young executive turned to experts to solve problems in the purchasing department. That process—seeking out the expert in the field—is part of the methodology of the professional manager. "There was trouble with purchasing," Tom explains. "The guy in charge was a kid who had been moved up—what did he know about purchasing? I kept saying, 'Let's get a professional, I'll get you a professional.' And the sales manager was screaming at the production manager because they were out of stock in so many places. I said, 'Take your back-order list and give everything a priority. Plan your sales for the next two months, and give them priorities.' I showed the list to the production manager and said, 'Can you get this out in sixty days at seventy percent of capacity?' He said, 'Yes.' 'Then stop yelling at each other every day.' "

In planning, too, the young executive found a deficiency in the small company. Tom's own inclination, the result of his education and big-company experience, was to draw up plans and set goals, but the smaller company was unused to that professional procedure. "I keep trying to get the president to operate on a plan," says the young executive. I say, 'Let's set out the policies we're going to have. Do you want a specialty house or the cheapest house? Now think about it, Ed, what do you want?' Maybe I can never teach him this process, but I've got to try, I've got to try."

The man conducting this finely balanced endeavor has neither suavity nor social polish. He is largely self-educated, and almost all of his experience is in accounting. He has adapted his abilities to meet the exceptionally fragile assignment he is now undertaking—carrying to that assignment his habitual independence of mind. "On the job before this one, I made a lot of friends," he says. "But I also stirred up a lot of people. I'm a little bit the stirring-up kind. If you don't say what's on your mind, nobody knows there's another side to the point. And when I'm hiring, I don't look for a man who just knows the rules. I'm interested in the misfit accountant."

Despite the stimulation of his present job, which would warrant the interest of a Metternich, Tom—in a manner characteristic of his generation—cannot imagine that he will continue to deal with it for a very long period of time. "I'm still waiting for a top management opportunity to come along," he remarks coolly. "I realize waiting is part of the game. I've stated my desires, and I know the job I'm looking for isn't always available—that makes me feel I should have a little patience. If a job offered to me somewhere else were developmental and creative, I guess I could be tempted away. I'd look long and hard at the top people. The egotistical genius type of management wouldn't suit me, and neither would the let's-wait-a-bit type. If a company had decided to go big internationally and was looking for somebody with my mixed bag of background I would listen. I'd be foolish not to. Right now, just a

$10,000 a year increase wouldn't interest me. Two years from now, if this new division is doing all right and nothing else has come along here—then, I'll be a prime target. But right now, I'm happy mending this little company."

That the young executive is confronted with so complicated a piece of needlework obviously comes about as a consequence of the size of the organization he works for. His big company had the strength to make the acquisition in the first place, and, because of its margin of abundance, it can afford the cost of the experiment of retaining the acquired company's founder. Within the framework of the policy decision that the older man should remain as president of the new division, the young executive has plenty of room for maneuver: the way he chooses to remake the thought patterns of a man twenty years his senior, how he constructs and reconstructs his relationships with that man and others in the division, how he keeps his superiors at home informed, how he seeks to avoid even hinting at authority while moving the division in the direction he wants it to go—that is his field for action. For all the decisions he makes within that field, this accountant need give no accounting. The only occasion that would require a full explanation would be his failure to bring the division, president and all, around the corner to profitability.

The process by which a corporation spins off a long-cherished subsidiary can be just as full of challenges to the young executive as the process of acquisition. Accomplishment of divestiture is just as hazardous, and the road is just as pot-holed, as the process of acquisition. In one case, both the rigorous alembic leading to a decision to divest and the conduct of much of the across-the-table negotiation were carried out by a man we shall name John, the top financial man for a major pharmaceutical house. John joined his company seven years ago, and at the age of thirty-seven he became one of the youngest treasurers of a major corporation in the United States. When John decided to convince his top management of the wisdom of spinning off a hairbrush division that had been part of his company for half a century, he started a long journey down a tricky path.

John's initial urge to move his company to this sale came out of that common wellspring of young executive action, "the good of the business." Relates John, in a much-used phrase, "I felt it would be best for the company." And, acting in a manner typical of his generation, John buttressed that feeling by spading up supporting data about immediate conditions and industry-wide circumstances. "Fifty percent of the hairbrush division's volume wasn't in brushes at all. It was in heavy plastics—refrigerators, cars, TV sets. Hairbrushes were only about twenty-five percent," John explains. "My opinion was that the plastics business was no place to be if you didn't integrate. We didn't own our own sources of supply. Our return on investment was dropping. You just couldn't stay in. In my view, by 1970 there won't be anyone in the plastics business who isn't integrated. The division was slowing down our over-all growth, it had very little profit, it was cyclical—I felt we were being hampered. We didn't want to get out of the hairbrush business, but in 1961 we had acquired Lactona, a small company that also made hairbrushes—that made it all the more imperative to spin off the old division. I said, 'Let's get out now, the squeeze has started.' "

Once he had examined his facts, and had come to his decision, John was bolstered by complete confidence in his own judgment. He never worried over his decision after that time. Instead, he turned his efforts to mustering support for his position, and to finding just the right degree of persistence required to achieve the objective—enough persistence so that the issue would not die, but not so much so as to defeat his purpose by stirring up resistances from the three layers of management above him. "Of course the sale meant taking away $20 million in sales and some profit," says John. "Sometimes it takes more courage to spin off than to acquire. But I never had a moment's doubt. I fought for the sale for a long time. I suppose there were times when top management wished that I would shut up, but I didn't shut up.

"For two years I didn't get anyplace. But I pushed for what I thought was best for the corporation. I could tell that the chief executive didn't want to face up to the sale of the business, because he is very conscious of people. He was very upset at the thought of what might happen to them. He insisted that there wouldn't be any sale if the people weren't going to be well off. We would not sell to a marginal company or one that would not continue the fringe benefits. Identical benefits or better, that was to be in the contract."

John did not hesitate to disagree with the opinions held by others in the organization about the sale. He regarded such disagreement as an objective part of the business situation, and he kept it untinged with emotion. "While the decision to sell was being considered," he recalls, "we spent a whole day with the division's management team. We talked things over with them very carefully. We saw their five-year projections. We felt they were too optimistic. We didn't tell the division chief what our intentions were then. We felt that by keeping him in the dark we could give him a better opportunity outside—to associate him with the hard preliminary negotiations might have embarrassed him with his new employers later on. We felt we could drive a harder bargain if we left him out of it. And we would be better off in the end, we felt, because his new employers could do so much more with the business. When he was told what we were thinking, he disagreed with the sale. He told the chief executive why he thought we should stay in this business. He never showed any antagonism. But I'm sure he was angry."

In the end, persistence was capped with a stroke of positive daring that settled the matter. "When I saw we weren't being successful in pushing for a decision, I'd drop the matter of the sale for a while. Every couple of months, I would bring it up again—each time with more ammunition. Finally, the thing that got it off the ground was finding a buyer. I found the buyer. I went to the chief executive and said, 'Well, here I am again; here's a buyer.' I knew I could get into trouble. I had my neck out a mile. But I felt we had to take the initiative," John says.

"The buyer was an outstanding company. Our general counsel and I handled the negotiations for the sale, taking half the sale price in the stock of the company we sold to. The appreciation on that stock since then has been greater than the profits of the division for three or four years. I was convinced that the stock was going to go up. It was a good deal for the acquiring company because they can bring to the division things that we couldn't. And the people working in the division are going to be better off. I really think it's better for everybody. We'd still be concerned, though, if lots of our old divisional people were fired. We're one of the acquiring company's largest stockholders; we'd be very upset. Actually, I think we could keep it from happening. Anyway, I don't think the problem will come up."

John found personal gratification in the conduct of the close negotiations. They helped him to become what he wants always to become—a more knowledgeable and efficient operator. "I took great personal pleasure in all this, as well as knowing that it was a good thing for the company. The fellow negotiating with us was a real crackerjack. It was really stimulating. I learned a lot. I benefited for future negotiations. When you get a dumb buyer or seller—well, he has no idea of the value of the business, he costs himself money, the situation deteriorates. It makes you lax. But with the smart ones—they put you on your toes, you learn you may not be as smart as you think. You make sure you aren't overlooking any details. It broadens your thinking."

As a professional, John watches the acquisition and sale of companies constantly. He studies each case for what he can learn from it, tries to puzzle out the good moves and the bad ones, sharpens his own professional skill. Says he: "We have no single competitor, we have many. One of them is extremely tough. They're often willing to pay more for a company than we feel it's worth. We have lost things we wanted to that company, but not at the price they paid. We had a shot at one acquisition before they did. We evaluated it and decided what it was worth, but we and the seller were miles apart so we left it. Our competitor finally got it at a price closer to the seller's than to ours. One usually ends up knowing what price was paid, even when it isn't published—you get a feel for it, just by talking around. Maybe we were wrong about the one we didn't buy. If we were, you can give the mistake to me. A man has to be more right than wrong, but he's entitled to his mistakes. The man who doesn't make them isn't doing anything."

Like all young executives, John muses occasionally over the possibility that he might leave his present company. That meditation does not come from any unhappiness—indeed, he expresses pleasure with his job and his employer—but from the self-analysis and awareness of opportunity that men like him constantly carry with them as they move ahead. "I ask myself sometimes, if I had to leave here for any reason, what I would do. If this company started in a direction that was completely wrong, I'd leave. Then I wouldn't hesitate to take a post like this in another large company . . . and I guess if I had an opportunity to be president of a small company, I might take it—" but as always, "for the challenge," not for the money alone. "You reach a point where financial remuneration doesn't mean as much as the chance to do things. It isn't the buck that triggers me at this moment. It's what you're doing, what you can create, what you see in the future."

Acquisition and spin-off are two manifestations of change in the world of big companies. A third manifestation is the special kind of association that big companies have with big customers: like the companies themselves, customers may be giants whose demands are special, whose positions are powerful, whose control over their suppliers is considerable. The greatest of these is the government. More than any other big buyer, the government can entangle the business situations that it enters. With the huge entity of government as his sole customer, and a great corporation as his employer, one would expect to find the young manager pressed flat as a bookmark between the two. To cope with such great forces, surely, would make him into the prototype of the organization man.

But it does not. While he may find the texture of his professional life a bit strange, the young executive who straddles those two worlds also finds it an engaging life, which muzzles neither his personality nor his actions. One such man is the manager of a big company's effort in missiles and space, who has two layers above him in the company hierarchy. Shifts in the strategy of the space age have led this man, whom we shall call Don, to witness both boom and turn-down at the installation he runs. Don, a top engineer and a top manager, was running that effort during the huge beginnings of the space program in 1959. And he was still there during 1962 and 1963, when the government canceled several major contracts, in each of which his division had an important interest. Don recalls the period since the cancellations as "a very sporty couple of years."

Explaining the cancellations, Don says: "These are large and complex programs. It takes three years or more before these spacecraft are ready to fly. By that time, everybody has learned so much that some things that used to look good seem like a waste of time. That's the main reason why contracts are canceled. On some of the contracts we lost, we were not entirely blameless. If our performance had been perfect we might have survived. While the work was going on, we tried to generate an awareness through the organization that we were doing things that had never been done before. But there are literally 20,000 to 30,000 parts in one of these spacecrafts. And there's absolutely no margin for error. We ran into difficulties—although the contracts might have been cut off anyway." Loss of one of the contracts, however, did not worry Don too much, because, like other young executives, he puts a good deal of emphasis on learning: "Actually, we didn't shed a tear when one of them was lost. They wanted everything to be proven parts, so there wasn't a new thing in it. We weren't learning anything. But we hated to lose one of the others—it had tons of opportunity."

With the cancellation of the contracts, Don had to face a

new kind of activity for him—trimming back an operation that had done nothing but grow since the day it was born. Don says, "We were doing $150 million to $200 million a year. Take out those programs, and we were left facing 1963 with a lot of excess capacity." But the need to cut back also had its brighter side for Don. It appealed to him, as it would to many other managers like him, as an opportunity to run a tighter operation—a chance to experience the pleasure of making improvements in efficiency. "Actually, this reduction did the place a lot of good," Don says. "Life had been getting too easy. We had been getting contracts hand over fist, and taking on too many of them."

"Our first problem," Don continues, "was to cut overhead to fit lower volume, so that we could be competitive." At one plant Don had to cut back from 11,000 to 8,000 employees—a distasteful job that he took on with swift adjustment to the new facts. On the need for that cut-back, he comments with typical realism: "There was a clear picture of alternatives. It meant a problem for 3,000 people, but if we didn't get the overhead in line, it might have meant the whole business."

Big government and big business are supposed to be shot through with stability lovers and security seekers. But no man running his own shoe store on a corner of Main Street ever faced more uncertainty than Don does in his business endeavors. For all the size of the forces he deals with, he knows something about life on the razor's edge. "This year a specially important satellite is due to fly," Don says. "It's really going to be a moment of truth. In my opinion it has had a lousy managerial setup. I'm fearful how it will turn out. We could only get meager information about the size and weight of the power system, yet we had to design the craft. As trouble developed, we weren't allowed to fix it. Instead we had to send the pieces back, there was an endless back and forth. Something goes wrong in the cabling. We send it back. They bring it back and say it works. . . . If it doesn't work we'll get blamed. Yet we really have no control over it. Once it's up there, no one can touch it to adjust it. Yet we're staking our professional future on this. If it's a flop, I may not be here next year. We catch a lot of errors, but I keep worrying, do we catch 'em all? You live with this bomb over you month after month."

The stress of change also puts pressure on Don in other ways. He responds by re-examining what were once lapidary first premises, to see if they still have validity. A good example is the current state of what a few years ago was the latest sensation of the space age—the space simulators whose black interiors reproduced the conditions of outer space, with its vacuum and its cryogenic temperatures. Space vehicles suspended and rotating in the belly of the globe faced the same kind of stresses that they would meet in outer space. But now the mission of the space vehicle lasts so much longer than was anticipated then that the space simulator is already obsolescent. "Because it costs so much to put a vehicle into orbit, we used to be able to go through ground testing of the same duration as the mission time," explains Don. "But now the time the space vehicle is supposed to spend in space is much longer, and we sometimes have as much trouble keeping the test equipment running as we do with the spacecraft. We have a lot to learn about operating this test equipment—and unless it's more reliable than the spacecraft you are testing, it's a losing battle."

Those new conditions seemed to give rise to the once unheard-of possibility that it might be cheaper to orbit the spacecraft than to test it for prolonged periods of time on the ground before launching. But still another change is intervening: boosters, since they must have greater capacities, cost more than they did before, with the consequence that more expenditure on test equipment may be warranted. But even this may not be the case for very long. Indeed, in Don's business life, nothing is the way it was for very long, and he maintains a perennial willingness to give new situations a fresh look.

These four exemplary situations we have looked at have a good deal in common. Each of them was carried on against a big-company backdrop: the milieu was the great corporation. Against that backdrop, we have seen the young executive dealing with the delicate fretwork of business situations: the making of a president, the merging and the renewal of obsolete facilities, the sale of an ebbing company, the adaptation to the needs of the great customer in the space age. But in none of these situations was the man cast into a corporate mold. He did not have to conform in any important way to any prearranged patterns of behavior.

Listen to Them Talk

Does the young executive abhor personal responsibility? On the contrary, he wants it very badly—so badly that he hates to admit that the play of mere chance can defeat him. When he is beaten, he looks for the cause of the defeat within himself, or in external circumstances that, had he acted differently, he might have controlled. One young executive recollects a bit of past drama:

"I never believed, even when I was in athletics in college, in being a good loser. I wanted to win. I remember once in the last game of the year, for the championship, when we had three yards to go for the winning score. I was captain and quarterback. I called the run-pass option, the play that had been our best ground-gainer all season. I took the ball, and rolled out to my right, with good blocking. As I ran, I could see that a defensive back was the only one with a chance to stop me. I might have beaten him in a footrace . . . then I looked to the left, and saw my favorite pass-receiver, all alone in the end zone, waving his arms. I passed. The ball went chest-high, right into his hands. He dropped it, and we lost. Later on everybody told me to forget it, we had a great year anyway. But I'll never forget it. Instead of keeping the ball and going for the distance myself, I passed—I choked. I passed the responsibility to someone else instead of keeping it—that's what hurts."

Hand in glove with that sense of responsibility goes the young executive's confidence in his ability to handle responsibility once he has got it. In an incident that displays confidence very forcefully, another young executive recalls a youthful decision:

"I left one company because I felt my mind wasn't being stretched enough on the job. I was twenty-seven at the time. I

went to the executive vice-president of the company to resign. A few days later he called me into his office. He said: 'Look, I've talked to the president about this. This isn't the kind of thing we usually say, and there can't be any promises about it. But we think you may be president of this company someday. I'll never make it, I'm fifty-five now. But you may. So when you think about leaving, consider that.' I know it sounds ridiculous for a man of twenty-seven, but here's what I said to him: 'I've always assumed I could get to be president. If I didn't assume that I would have left a long time ago. But what I've decided is that this job just isn't interesting enough. Being president wouldn't satisfy me.' I guess it was a pretty egotistical thing to say. I know he was startled. But that was honestly the way I felt about it, and I left."

Chapter SIX

The Man and His Style

His abilities and his drive make the young executive a much sought-after business commodity. A professional manager between the age of thirty and forty-five, who has made his way successfully through big-company ranks, and who stands now on the upper slopes of corporate management, he is a man forever stoking an inner fire. As we have seen, the young executives are pressing men: they press perpetually toward external accomplishment, toward winning certain trappings of success, toward deeper and deeper immersion in their business careers. They are possessed by what one of them has called "the burn"—a driving impulse that may make them hard men to live with, but leaves them happy living with themselves as long as there is accomplishment to look back on, and promise to look forward to. Their performance, their standards, their wells of pleasure, and above all their style—the cut of their business jib, the way they move in and out of complicated big-company problems, their way of listening and talking intently, their occasional attitudinizing—these distinguish them from the rank and file manager, and these mark them for more promotion to come.

To this special man, responsibility has become an almost organic thing. The young executive has seen his responsibility grow steadily in the course of his business career. Its enlargement provides the key to his interest, or better to his submergence, in his work. For every increase in responsibility brings him changes: a new locus of action, a new focus of endeavor, a whole new business horizon to explore. It is primarily to

98

have the pleasure of struggling with such changes, and of solving the problems that they bring, that the man wants to be promoted. Every promotion carries to him what he calls "new challenges"—new means of whetting his intellectual appetite.

That appetite is very restricted. Only the meat of business can feed it. The young executive's intellectual curiosity rarely extends beyond the confines of his job. He is a man who communicates best with other businessmen, who proceed from the same premises and have the same vocabulary. But we have noted that he has not made himself well understood by other groups in our society: academicians, for example, who have their own kind of narrowness, have little conversance with the true nature of business and business decisions, and the young executive must bear his share of responsibility for the mutual lack of understanding. It is a rare man among this generation of young executives who engages in intellectual pursuits outside the world of business.

But the young executive's restricted intellectual appetite is also very intense. He is a greedy man—greedy not for money, but for big and little facts about his business. He likes to study and re-study those facts, lest he wrongly assume that they are eternal: as one of them says, "There's a real tendency for people to remember and use as facts things that today just aren't facts any more. I find myself falling into that trap. I may think 'Item A is a fact' just because it was a fact seven years ago. Then I start to wonder whether it still is a fact." The young executive wants to be objective in his evaluation of the meaning of fact. And, contrary to the myths that surround him, this man likes to be outspoken in his discussions about business situations with colleagues and superiors; indeed it would be impossible for him to be anything else, since there is no other way that his hard-won knowledge of the facts can be put to use. When decisions are made, he likes them to be made on the merits of the given situation—prejudice may enter other parts of his life, but he tries to keep it out of his business decisions. And he looks for a similar disinterested posture on the part of his colleagues.

All this imparts to the young executive his big-company style. His power as a manager for a big company has its frontiers, mapped out by company policy, but within those frontiers, the young executive is accustomed to the right to cultivate the terrain in his own way. He wants and takes and wields as much within-the-walls authority as he can get; sometimes he even pushes the walls outward a bit. His work is complicated by the fact that, like most members of his group, he is a professional who feels impelled to meet not only the standards set by his company, but also the outside standards of his profession, whatever it may be. Those standards create some inner conflicts from time to time. But an even greater conflict comes when the young executive, who is a citizen by birth in big-company country, moves to another land. There he may find that the tenets he believes in do not obtain. Business decisions may be arrived at in ways other than the ones he knows—and he finds he likes these other kinds of processes far less. Often he is confronted with either compromising with his beliefs, or getting out—and going back to the atmosphere more congenial to him, back where, as he never tires of saying, "there's a chance to do things." That is his element.

Big business fashions much of the character of our society. While they rarely articulate the thought, the young executives get some of their satisfaction from their participation in big business—from helping to shape the element which, in turn, shapes many of our social patterns. Some of these men, who have lived all their business lives in big companies, express an occasional, half-romantic desire to "run my own apple stand" —but, on more careful consideration, they usually retreat from the thought, largely because, as one of them puts it, "It would be just that—just an apple stand." They have cultivated a taste for bigger things.

A kind of big-number fascination figures as part of that taste. The young executive usually deals in millions, and he relishes the fact. One young man who works for a copper company obviously enjoys having played an important role in the design and introduction of a cost-cutting program that, in the end, will save his company some $75 million—big enough in anybody's book. Another who comes from a poor family— "I was baptized by immersion into some of the tougher aspects of life"—reports that one of his earliest ambitions was to run his own store. He tingles a little now when he says: "Now, I'm doing it—multiplied 1,500 times. We have 1,500 retail outlets. The problems are fantastic. A woman gets pinched or a store gets looted and there I am, in the middle of it with the store manager. Some of the situations couldn't be more difficult— always a crisis. But I feel like I'm master of my own destiny."

A Chase Manhattan executive echoes this theme. He waves away the suggestion that he might be happier running a bank of his own. "I already feel as though I'm running the biggest bank in New York—130 banks, in fact," he says. Another man explains that one of the reasons he stays with his present employer is "because of the way we're growing. In a few years, we'll be a billion-dollar company"—a figure, obviously, which has its magic for him. And the financial vice-president of one conglomerate, who is now thirty-four, recalls that when he was with another company, and still in his twenties, he elicited oral five-year plans from division managers and then "went back to my office and converted their plans into numbers. When that report was presented to the First National Bank, we got a $45-million loan"—a sizable beginning for this man's sizable experience with big numbers.

Flavor is added to the young executive's life by subtle relationships that he must maintain with hordes of people in his big company. He delights in, and also is exasperated with, his constant tramps through this reedy ground. Whether the people he deals with are subordinates or not, they usually cannot be moved—at least not in the right direction—by authoritarian means. In the young executive's own overworked words, he must always try to "motivate people"—by which he means that he must incite those around him to want to act, and sometimes to think, the way that he wants them to act and think. Here the man dwells in a slippery and shadowy region, where results are not so easily measured as they are in an overt action to solve an external problem; but it remains a vitally important area for today's managers. Every businessman, of course, has people to deal with; but the managers in large companies are involved with others to a higher-pitched and sometimes extremely trying degree. "It always comes down to the same old thing—people," is a reiterated cry of the young executive. The abilities of the people around him constitute one of his greatest resources; how to swing that resource into effective action constitutes one of his greatest and most intriguing difficulties.

Along with the young executive's talent for maneuvering people and his fondness for big numbers goes his appreciative cognizance of what big companies can accomplish. Often he works with a big company because, as he says, big companies "can do so much more." The young executives are sometimes hemmed in by what philosophers and social scientists have identified as the hardening tendency, and the tendency toward inertia, coming from the big organization. But they are also stimulated, and their business interest is heightened, by the knowledge that a big company can bear down with so much strength on a business situation. John Smith, at thirty-eight a group executive with a big electronics company, points out that "in a small business, I would have far fewer resources. In a big company, I can get more things done. And the major drive that managers have is to get things done, to see something happen." Smith is not unaware of the hazards that size can bring: "Religion was more dynamic when the early Christians were meeting in cellars. In the big churches today, it's harder to get hold of the basic tenets. And in big business, it's difficult to understand what it's all about." But that difficulty, for Smith, reduces itself to a problem on the job: "In a big company, you have to work extra hard to overcome that—to understand what is going on, and what the purposes are, and to see that people working for you understand those things. People can get satisfaction out of being a part, however small, of something important. In a utility, maybe a guy just reads meters but he gets satisfaction out of helping to supply all this power. It depends on a person's motivations."

Smith has not yet been introduced to the traditional organization man who believes that the best way to move ahead in the company is to avoid personal responsibility. On that point, he comments: "The people I know are concerned with having a clean line of authority and responsibility, with being given the opportunity to take the risks." Nor does Smith seek to hire the man who will accept imaginary limitations on his job chalked out by the top management of the company. "Considering a man for employment," he says, "we look for creativity. Is he willing to think differently? We'd take lesser qualities in other respects in order to have that. Sometimes we're in a real engineering spot, when we can't make something work. Then someone comes up with a whole new attack, twisting and turning the technical data. This happens every day. That's what we mean by creativity—new ways of doing the job."

Smith has a doctorate in electronic engineering, and part of his job is to keep a kind of surveillance over some of the research laboratories of his company. To keep those laboratories meshed with corporate purposes is a tricky task. Commenting on it, Smith says, "In the case of research scientists, you don't manage them, you observe them. But you try to expose them to what the company is doing and what the class of problems is. You can't tell a man, 'I want you to invent a thing with these specifications in six weeks'—but he's got to be put in general tune with what we're about as a company." As for Smith himself, change, accelerated by the size and strength of his company, gives him all the kicks he needs. "I'd be unhappy in a static industry," he says. "I like the dynamics of this field."

Thus the young executive finds augmented interest, keener taste, and grander possibilities in working for a big company. Of course he must report to his superiors. But he usually does that in his own style. And the necessity to report to them does not restrict him intolerably in the cultivation of his own garden—in the activity that holds magnetic attraction for him.

For ranking managers in big companies, there are rarely any hard and fast rules about when to report to the top. The young executive is usually free to make his own interpretation about when he should ask for his boss' approval. He is the one who decides when he must seek an endorsement for a contemplated action, and when he can stretch his own charter to cover the case at hand. Curiously enough, when he does stretch his own authority, he often does so as much out of a sense of duty as out of his natural aggressiveness and pugnacity. "I review every major decision with the president of my company," says one young manager in explanation. "But I'm the one who decides when the decision is major. There isn't any book of rules about it. I'm free to go as far as I like. But when I discuss something with the president, I try to avoid asking him to make my decision for me. I know he doesn't want to proffer an opinion without knowing how I feel first. So I tell him what decision I want, and get his approval."

Another manager, three layers from the top in General Electric, enlarges on the point as he explains how he conducts his relationship with his immediate superior. "I minimize requests on my boss for a decision," he says. "If I ask him to make my decisions all the time, then he doesn't need me. I don't want him to worry about sharing what I've got to decide. I don't feel that would be fair to him. That's my responsibility." Still another executive, at the second level of management in I.T.T., recalls making a long swing through Latin America, changing and repairing the condition of half a dozen of his big company's subsidiaries. Never in the course of the trip did he refer any matter to his chief executive for a decision. "He knew in general what I was doing," says this man. "I didn't see any point in bothering him. He had enough other things on his mind without having to worry about my problems. I figured I could take care of those." In all his negotiations in Latin America, this manager heard from his boss only once: "All I ever heard from him was a two-line cable referring to one contract and saying, 'Be sure you don't allow the competition to offer more than we do.' Actually, I had already taken care of that point."

But in most cases the decision about when to seek the boss' seal of approval is secondary in interest and importance. The critical decisions are the ones connected with the solution of the problem at hand. Those problems are often impressive in their size and scope, and as he deals with them the young executive shows himself to be assured and confident. The thrust of decision comes from him, and from men like him throughout the business community; their decisions seem to explode upward from the middle and the upper-middle ranks. The young executive takes on assignments whose size would be beyond the ability of a small company to delegate, and whose composition is complicated by many considerations that smaller companies would not have to bother to weigh. The intricacy of those assignments, and the knowledge that he has so much influence over their outcome, is the source of the young executive's surface woes—and his deeper joys.

A good example may be found in the work of a young manager, Jack D., who works in the upper-middle ranks of a big international oil company. The sheer volume of business done in the department is enormous. It sells hundreds of thousands of barrels of crude oil a day, and its dollar volume last year ran to hundreds of millions. Jack, who is not yet forty, makes an individual contribution to the matters on which his department works whose importance varies with many factors. But whether the individual role he plays is large or small, Jack seems to find considerable personal gratification in it.

One of the most important functions of Jack's department is to determine the price at which crude should be sold. Recently Jack played a small role—one that he describes as "just peripheral"—in a very important pricing question: the determination of the price that his company should post for a newly discovered crude, which has gushed profusely on the international market in the last couple of years. The whole matter was so involved and cut across so many organizational lines that even the contribution of the entire department in which Jack works, which had the chief responsibility, was only a part of the total effort. Explaining the complexity of the problem, Jack says "This crude was intended for the refineries of Europe. But it contains more gasoline than the European market requires, and it gives an imbalance of products. It also contains a fair amount of wax, and refineries have to be well planned to handle it—all that tended to depress the price. But this crude has a low sulfur content, which is good. And it's near the market. We had to evaluate its worth to customers, the value to us, and we had to know a lot about the refineries we wanted to sell to." The price for the crude was so important that it went to the company's top executive committee for final decision.

But individual satisfactions were not lost in this corporate effort. Jack has no feeling that, because his role was not the only one or even a very important one in the decision-making process, he was merely a negligible cog in a huge machine. He is able to find satisfaction in the fact that he did a good job in tandem with many others—a kind of freedom, after all, in a big society. And, characteristically, he takes pleasure in the fact that the price worked out primarily by his department, but also by other departments of the company, smoothly passed the scrutiny of the executive committee. Says he: "The price our department proposed went right through at the executive committee meeting. There was a good area of agreement." And he believes, with an eye to the results—another bit of evidence that the young executive is "result oriented"—that the decision his company finally reached on the matter was a good one: "The price has stayed at the level that we recommended." And he finishes his account of the affair with an objective admission: "Of course, that doesn't necessarily mean that it was the proper level." Then the note of confidence: "But I'm convinced it was."

In his dealings with foreign governments, Jack has had a larger individual role to play. A petroleum engineer by trade, he has found fascination in sessions like the one he conducted not long ago with officials of a country we shall name Kubistano. A new refinery, in which his company had an investment, had just started up there. Jack was meeting with Kubistano officials to discuss the price at which his company was offering to sell its crude to the refinery. Usually fiercely competitive ("I play to win") and full of confidence ("I just don't get butterflies easily"), Jack admits to some nervousness as he began his talks: "Oil pricing is not very easy to talk about." And a good deal depended on the outcome: "It wasn't just head-to-head with a customer, it was also head-to-head with competitors. The Kubistano government had heard that it could buy crude at a lower price."

Jack began on a low key. "I tried to put myself in their place. I spent a good deal of time talking about pricing and giving some background on what the terms meant. I tried to demonstrate that the price we offered was a fair price—which indeed it was. Talking about other offers, I explained that naked price was not the only thing. We'd made an investment in Kubistano's refinery. The quality of the crude we offered fitted the refinery better, and therefore it represented a smaller foreign exchange drain. Our crude balances well, it has a high percentage of middle distillates and kerosene, which Kubistano needs more than industrial fuel and gasoline. If they ran a different crude, they would get products they couldn't dispose of. They couldn't get any crude the same quality as ours at a lower price. What I was trying to demonstrate, really, was how you assess the value of crude oil. The officials of the country were sophisticated and approachable and receptive. I like to talk to people like that. And I do think we gave them some information that will be useful to them in the future. I don't know anything I got more gratification from."

Later Jack moved on to another international undertaking of a similar degree of interest. He was sent to an Oriental country to regularize crude oil sales there. Jack went there with a frank awareness of his own limitations in the field: "I didn't have much of an understanding of what the market was like for fuel oil there. I had misgivings about my ability to do the job." But they were short-lived. "At the time, these people were already our customers," recalls Jack. "They were buying from us in the Middle East, but cargo by cargo. We wanted to get them under contract. That weds you to a customer, and makes it easier to plan. In the end I signed four companies to a long-term contract. We've been serving them on a contract basis ever since. We've sold more than we would have on a cargo basis—so we've done a better job of meeting their needs. And by being able to plan, we're able to cover them, even though we have a tight situation now. That's one of our objectives—to build security into our business."

Jack honestly believes that the contracts he and his colleagues negotiated with those two countries are good for the interests of both. But inseparable from his feeling of satisfaction is the knowledge that his contracts turned a profit for his company. If the profit element were not present, his whole response would be different. "It's satisfying to bring home the bacon. My feeling of satisfaction is not separate from the knowledge that we made a profit. I wouldn't have gotten any satisfaction out of the contracts if we hadn't made money." But with typical realism Jack points out the limitations of the profit possibility: "Sure it's a good idea to come back with the best deal you can. But it has to be realistic for the customer. He has to operate at a profit, too. I'm happy if I can get five cents more. On the other hand, if it's twenty cents more, I know it can't last, it doesn't make sense."

In what is for the generation of young executives a rather rare glance at broad considerations, Jack adds: "We do business fairly—maybe because of morals, maybe just because we're in the limelight. Oil has been international for a long time. It has been the subject of the most venal type of ranting. We in a big company are right out in front. I believe what we are doing is right. If we can't make our way of doing business stick, then the whole free enterprise concept is done."

A professional in the oil industry, Jack has a good deal of trouble envisioning circumstances that would cause him to leave it. "I've been through some tough times in this industry," he says. "I left Philadelphia just before they closed it down. I had some pangs about that. And I was at New Orleans when they laid off half the work force. I've had two jobs shot out from under me—not the kind of thing you like to go through. But even if things went sour in this industry for an extended period of time, I'd probably stick it out." Looking over his personal timetable of progress, Jack finds that, even with his own highly competitive spirit, he is well satisfied: "My progress here has suited me fine. Any concerns have been on the side of 'Do I deserve it?' 'Has it been too fast?'" He cares about his salary, of course, but it concerns him more as an index of progress than as a means of exchange: "I never asked for a raise. I never felt there was any justification in asking for one. But if I deserved one and didn't get it, I would bring up the issue—just to find out what the problem was. I don't want to stay where I'm not wanted."

To leave his present company on account of money seems as remote to Jack as it does to most other young executives. He is far more interested in the field he gets for action, in the external accomplishments that he can aim at and point to. But like many other professional managers, he would leave if he came to the conclusion that his ideas about the principles of good management were being violated. "I've been approached by other companies. But I have a little difficulty in seeing any more opportunity than I have where I am. But I would leave this company if I lost confidence in the people I was working for—I don't mean one boss, but if I lost confidence that this company was being well managed. That would be as compelling as the feeling that they didn't want me. I think I'd pack up then." But a warranted criticism of his work, however unkind, would probably not drive him away: "Oh, I've had my tail chewed more than once here. I don't think you can live without making mistakes. But I've never been unfairly criticized. On balance, everything I see is favorable."

Listen to Them Talk

Is he crushed by huge anonymous forces he cannot control? *"Dealing with the government doesn't grind me down. I see lots of frustration in it sometimes. But so far I've been able to adjust. Things just do take time. I'm content as long as I see that things are progressing, and someone isn't getting ahead of me."*

Does he have to say what the bosses want to hear? *"Life is too short to stay where there isn't mutual respect. I want to work in a climate of approval. The bosses I've had—most of them favor the rebel, the guy who wants to be independent. They like to be argued with. Nothing would make my present boss madder than to have me say, 'I did it because I thought you wanted me to.'"*

How tight are those company handcuffs? *"Sometimes I feel they have me in this job for only one reason, that I can do it better than anyone else at the moment. If the spectrum goes from enormous and everlasting loyalty to the company at one end to no really deep obligation on the other—well, I've had all those feelings at one time or another. In balance I guess I favor the latter—although I'd be crushed if one of my guys felt that way.*

"The possibility of failure doesn't enter my mind. Falsely or not, I have a feeling I could always land on my feet somewhere, doing this kind of work and enjoying it. I know I can't stay here forever. I'll have to move on in the company. New things like this are done by young peo-

ple. *Another fifteen years and I'll be an old fuddy-dud. I have to make room for others. The interest in growing is to give people opportunity—you can attract and hold better people that way. Except for that, I'm not too concerned about growth."*

Chapter SEVEN

The Man and the Secret Sharer

The young executive has a very distinctive company style that characterizes his movements and makes them congruous with his times and his objectives. Part of that style includes respect for standards that have their origins outside the walls of his company. To meet those standards is for the young executive, in an eerie kind of way, a little bit like suddenly coming face to face with another part of himself. That other self—like the pajamaed stowaway in Conrad's *Secret Sharer*—is his professional counterpart, the part of the young executive that belongs to a professional group. It is that part of him that believes in a wider business ethic. The group may be a formal society, like a society of engineers or a bar association, or a loose body that may never meet, like some fraternal order of salesmen or buyers. But whatever it is, membership in it keeps complicating the man's life by introducing outside professional standards that he feels compelled to measure up to. He usually cannot disregard them for long without hearing the admonitory voice of the secret sharer.

To one young executive who hears that voice, its sound is louder than any the boss can make. He is a man who sent a shipment of merchandise to an outfit that went bankrupt—with considerable loss to his company,—and who thinks that he made a professional blunder. "Our company president says that it was one of those external events that no one could anticipate, and that it's nobody's fault. I think that is generous of him. But I don't agree. If I had consigned the merchandise instead of selling it, we wouldn't be stuck like this. I just didn't give the matter enough deep thought. No matter what the president says, I blame myself."

Sometimes his loyalty to a separate set of values can cause the young executive plenty of anguish. Some men resign as a result of it. Others sustain the anguish, and ride out the storm. "I remember when I was a lowly factory accountant around here," recalls a man who is now an assistant treasurer. "We had a new production manager who wanted to make labor costs look lower. He was a vice president and he was infiltrating my department. Who was going to win—the v.p. or the junior accountant? I had hired some good men from the colleges and I had some commitment to them. I couldn't leave the company then. I made just one pronouncement: 'Costs shall be recorded for what they are and where they are incurred.'

"I struggled for two years to make that pronouncement stick. If you were the kind who got ulcers, you got one then and I got mine. We all had to hope and pray for this man's time to run out before our stomachs did. We had to realize that it was a period that had to be waited out. We instinctively knew that if we had the lasting power, the situation would right itself. You had an obligation to your own people, and another to top management—which was not this man's breed of cat. I had a sort of blind faith that it would end. Money wasn't involved. The biggest thing that kept me on was the fact that I had faith that this was not the way the company would be." That faith was eventually vindicated: "In the end, this vice-president ran into trouble and he resigned." To ride out the storm was a good decision: "Now we don't have any real politics. You can trust your boss and your people. You can feel comfortable with the quality of your superiors." And then the final, pragmatic justification: "The atmosphere is encouraging now, if you're the type who likes to do things."

Another man in a different activity expresses the same consciousness of outside standards. In this case, the man has developed his occupational conscience despite the fact that he never attended any formal professional school. Yet, as a purchasing agent for a big company, he had as much professional loyalty as a lawyer or an accountant. He takes considerable pleasure from the fact that he negotiated for his company the annual purchase of $1,500,000 worth of a chemical at an excellent price. "You get a kick out of a job well done like that," he says. "The junior buyer gets the same kind of kick out of the proper purchase of ten pounds of celery seed." But the same man, as a professional, is deeply troubled by his conviction that his company should be making, instead of buying, another chemical that it uses in volume. "Management says the timing is bad, that we don't have the ability, that we can't spare any engineers. I'm extremely frustrated. I can't seem to get my point across even though I've *made* the point. They just haven't given it sufficient review. I intend to keep resubmitting it."

This man is completely untroubled by the thought that top management may become annoyed at his stubbornness. The old organization man would of course have retreated fearfully rather than risk incurring organizational wrath, or upsetting the organization's managerial patterns. But today's young executive reacts quite differently: "I'm not worried about whether they'll get tired of hearing from me or not," he says frankly. "I just don't think enough attention has been given to my study. The market demands that we do this now. I'm not satisfied that we can't break away some of the engineering talent we've got. In a smaller company I'd have another point of view, but in our size company, no. It troubles me because it's costing us money, and I can't justify that as against saving engineering talent. I think we're just taking the easy way out. In today's market, we could reap a good profit by making this. I'm unable to see the other side of it. I want a vice-president to explain to me why we can't make it." Then he expresses in a phrase what might well be regarded as one of the maxims of his generation of managers: "I don't demand love," he says.

But while professional standards can trouble a man's thoughts, and perhaps his dreams, on the one hand, they can also flavor his pleasures on the other. One engineer in the upper ranks got a deep kind of engineering-managerial gratification out of his recent and successful completion of a company project. A wave of change gave David G., thirty-eight, an executive with a tractor maker, his opportunity in the first place. A big tractor plant was being redesigned, and the spray-paint equipment in it being pulled out—offering David and a group of engineers a chance to substitute a painting process that would be more effective and economical. "This was all part of a plant reorganization," says David. "Spray painting was coming out anyway, and we decided to study what would be best as a replacement."

The study began with a survey of methods used in the company's other plants. "One of our subsidiaries in Britain was using electrostatic painting," says David. "We considered this too. But we finally had to shoot it down. The savings that apply in Britain don't apply in Kalamazoo. In Britain paint costs more than it does here, and labor costs less." Finally David and his group settled on a new process, flow-coat painting—in David's words, "a waterfall of paint that you run parts through, instead of spraying them. It's a tricky process—there are so many different parts of so many different sizes and shapes that unless flow-coat painting is done right, they all come out dripping paint all over the place—it's a mess. Other plants had failed in this way. But their engineering wasn't right."

To make it work David and his group came up with a radical new design. "We built a paint tunnel twice as long as any ever built before. We're putting a fantastic variety of parts and thicknesses through it." David gets an engineering lift out of the new departure: "It's working, and it's unique in the country," he says. But there is a manager's pleasure in it, too: "There's a 50 percent paint saving, and it's faster—parts move through the paint at ten feet a minute. The paint unit cost $500,000. The saving in paint is $50,000 a year, although that wasn't the major consideration."

Because of the earlier failures, David and his associates did not find a ready reception when they went to top management with the flow-coat suggestion. "When we presented our proposal to the executive vice-president, he was reluctant to hear it," remembers David. "He knew about those early failures, and he asked a great many questions. But in the end he was receptive."

The young executive's big-company style suits him very well while he is living in the big-company atmosphere. But when man and style are transplanted to another milieu—a small company, or even a big one that is retrograde in its managerial policies—the young executive is often unpleasantly surprised. He may find that the tacit operating principles which he has always accepted as part of the natural order of things are not so widely followed as he thought. Under those uneasy circumstances, he may try, with varying degrees of success depending on the man, to rationalize away his discontents. Or he may quit, and go back to the atmosphere he understands better and finds himself more at home in.

One such situation presents itself in the account of a man who works in a company that has outgrown its founder, and become a big corporation—but, because of the grip the founder still keeps on the organization, it still has a small-society syndrome. Companies with those qualities exude a special aura that can have its effect on a professional manager in their ranks: among those managers who stay on with such companies, judgments and attitudes may warp, and unhappy compromises be made. Listen, for example, to the recollections of this man as he relates how the decision to build a new plant was arrived at in his big but strangely immature company: "The boss decided last year that we ought to make a product similar to our old one, but in a higher-priced line," he says. "I knew that would mean lots of engineering. I asked exactly what kind of product he had in mind. He said, 'I don't know, set up the plant and then we'll decide.' I wasn't in a position to debate about the plant, it was a demand. There were no plans, no budget, no nothing. I couldn't hire trained people, because I didn't know whether I could afford to pay the higher salaries." After a long struggle, this man finally had a plant operating. "Then I had to push this high-priced product," he says. "There was one man in our company who didn't want to handle it. He was afraid of it. So I went to the boss, and he pushed this product down this man's throat."

Jurisdictional lines in such situations become obscure. No one but the boss really has the authority to decide anything. Changes are made largely at the whim of the chief executive. "In one job I was sales manager. I had nothing to do with our local factory. Then I get a call from the boss who says, 'I want you to tell production to get out a shipment of bushings to Ballard next week.' I asked, 'Are you saying that I can tell people who don't work for me what to do?' He said, 'Yes.' So I got the stuff out." The responses of the men in charge of production are not recorded.

To innovate intelligently in this kind of corporate soil is a near-impossible task. "We have certain lines I would like to discontinue," complains this young manager. "But the boss doesn't want to close them down. They mean prestige to him. Of course the boss isn't God; he could be wrong." But because of the boss' conduct in another realm, which would be totally irrelevant in a more mature business atmosphere, even the poor business decisions go unchallenged. "He doesn't run a $200,000 company yacht, after all. So we let him have the prestige he wants. Let him keep these product lines." Inevitably, any decision must be accompanied by the word of the chief executive to carry weight down the line: "The plant here has been doing things wrong, even though they promised to straighten out. Unless something is done quickly, I'm going to the boss." And access to the boss is the surest source of power: "I spend a lot of time decoding what he says, and saying it so people can understand it. I act as interpreter"—a position of considerable authority in this atmosphere.

Trivia take on great weight. "My people look on me as a victim; they think the boss doesn't really know what he is doing," admits this man. Since that view is so widely held, he must conduct his public relationships with the boss with extreme caution. "In front of a group of people who would have given their right arms to get into his limousine with him, I refused. I said I had something else I had to do. I didn't want the reputation of a guy who rides in limousines with the boss." Then the final comment: "Yet, you know, he's pretty good really," this man says without too much conviction. "He has a genius for organization." This young executive has not yet worked himself out of his discontent.

But the case is not typical. More typical is the disturbance of one manager who once worked for General Electric and then moved to a smaller company. He went there because he thought he saw more opportunity to get something done there —"by hindsight, a mistake." He chose a company that in his judgment "had, and still has, a terrific future in terms of products." But he soon found that the character of the management of the small company—and that meant the character of the boss—was a great disappointment. "I found this company weak in management," he says, "in the sense that it had a president who was independent in the extreme. I found a great difference in principles, mostly related to management."

This man's difficulties in the small company began soon after he began to operate in the only way he knew. Confidently, he began making his own decisions, assuming that his actions would find their own justification once the results were in. "I had a free hand for three months," he says, "and got my accomplishments done then. But after that it was very difficult." After making an early discovery, as he says, "that there was very little growth from within in this company," this manager characteristically made "a charter for myself" to correct this deficiency. He started by reorganizing the areas under his personal control—without worrying about approval for his actions, since he assumed that his authority naturally extended that far. "My division was relatively small, about $4,500,000 a year," he explains. "It had three main products, and I set up each one as an independent profit center. Research was buried when I got there. I began some major changes in that respect. I found one product that needed lots of promotion, so I put in an advertising budget for $400,000."

The consequence of this series of independent actions was immediate and explosive. "The boss hit the roof," recalls this man ruefully. "He was apoplectic. His favorite expression, which he assumed a phoney accent for, was 'Vat's dis?' " For his reply, the young executive fell back on what, according to his lights, should have been the invincible fortress—the facts of the case. "I tried to prove that we could generate a lot of profit—that this product I wanted to advertise heavily was really worth pushing." But the advertising budget looked too huge. Facts were useless in the face of a wave of emotion. "The boss said at first that he wouldn't approve the advertising budget unless he saw the advertising layout. But really, he didn't like the whole basic approach." And the boss refused even to render a flat and final veto: "All he said was, 'I'm giving you my decision. I'm not approving this now.' " Then he spent six months in Europe. And while he was away, the advertising agency called me up. I had to fish or cut bait. I really sweated that one out." But inevitably this man made his own kind of decision: "Finally, I took the bull by the horns. I told the agency to go ahead." He expected to be fired out of hand when the boss returned. But such direct action was not forthcoming. "When the boss got back he never said a word. But from then on it was a jab here, a jab there. He resented the fact that I had made the decision, but he never talked about it again."

Others in the company waged their struggles with the boss, too. But they were not accustomed to the habits of a big company; this made their adjustments easier. "I had a sales manager who would go in and pound the boss' desk. If he got thrown out three times, he knew the issue was dead. But if he got thrown out only twice, he thought that there was still a chance." A decision, a new look at the facts, a re-evaluation, another decision, later still another look—that is a process that the young executive understands and often initiates. But to come away from an interview with the boss with nothing learned but the degree of his emotional response to a suggestion or a plan was foreign to this man's nature. Speaking of his sales manager, this young executive admits: "He bounced a little better than I did."

This manager's basic disagreement with the boss came with the different weight that each of them gave to results. In the short period when the young executive had freedom of action, he had already made some material and demonstrable progress. He had great difficulty, therefore, in seeing the reason for all the objections to his action. "I wanted to operate as a separate entity," he says. "My point was that we could move faster that way. I got all the talent, I budgeted, I exceeded all the results we had agreed to. I hired a couple of good technical people at $15,000 a year—very hard to find at that price. Yet after I did that, the boss insisted on doing all the hiring himself." Finally the real difference in attitude, the deep cleavage between the two men, emerged. "I saw that he felt that his way of doing the job was more important than the results," recalls this man. "He had grand illusions about his management ability. And he was very adamant—he was not going to let me have my freedom."

The end came shortly after that discovery. Typically, the young executive went to his boss to invoke what to his mind should have been the indisputable principle—the good of the business. "I said, 'Look, I'm being hamstrung. And this isn't fair to you either. Your business is being hurt.'" When that appeal proved fruitless, says this man, "It was obvious what the situation was going to be. So I started looking around." Predictably, this man went back to a big company—not because he wanted more security, but because he wanted more freedom. Basically, what he had found intolerable was the surveillance and the gossip that is characteristic of a small society. Like other young executives, he is, metaphorically speaking, a big-city man.

These examples show the young executive responding to an alien environment. But when he is in his home country, his judgments are not thus refracted. There he can be dispassionate, studious, and effective. His work nurtures him, it provides his life with its intellectual center of gravity. As one young executive says, "When I'm on the job, I'm aroused." But he pays a price for the maintenance of that high pitch: "It takes time for me to adjust when I get home at night," he admits. "That's why the martini is so popular."

Listen to Them Talk

Ethical questions, in the complicated way in which they present themselves in business, have the glitter of fascination for the young executives. Some of their views on morality:

"One important part of my job is making sure that we do our buying with the highest ethical standards, and trying to develop controls that will show up the defects if it isn't done that way. We watch the ratio between the business a company does with us and its total business. Sometimes the business with us may go up to 70 percent or 80 percent. If it gets unduly high we know that the company is tempted to give gifts to the buyer and we know that the buyer is tempted to accept them. We go on the assumption that our buyers are honest. But we're also old enough to know that people can be tempted. We have gotten many compliments on the caliber of the buyers that we have here. We are just interested in perfection in this connection and we get intolerant when we don't have it."

Dwelling on the question of ethics, another young executive, highly educated in the field of finance, explains why he changed jobs:

"One day one of my colleagues stopped in my office and said, 'Look what I did'—he had just joined another company as executive vice-president. I spent many evenings with him after that trying to keep him and his new company from getting clobbered financially. I got involved. And just at that point my disillusionment with Pete, my old boss, was pretty high. It had been growing for about a year. It wasn't any personal disagreement—I never spent much time with him as a person. It was disagreement over facts. I decided he was immoral and unethical in many of the things he was doing. I didn't want to be associated with him anymore. I didn't leave for money—actually, my annual income after I left was less

than it had been. After the boss talked to a couple of people and found out that I was going to make less on the new job, he probably thought I was a damned fool. But I had to do it. I had found myself spending more and more time with this man on problems that were less and less important to the company. That way, you begin to hate yourself. People would talk to me about the boss and say, 'Isn't he wonderful?' I was expected to agree, but in fact I found myself in disagreement 90 percent of the time. It was impossible to be enthusiastic and affirmative."

A young executive in a big oil company talks a bit about what he cannot give:

"If I were ever encouraged or directed to do something distasteful to me, I'd leave. I don't mean dishonest—that's further down the road. I mean something that to me was unethical—even if it wasn't to someone else—or something that was deceitful, even if a lawyer said it was okay. If something like that came along, the company would just have to give. They would have to accommodate me. I can't accommodate in that area. There's only one way to take honesty and that's straight out of the bottle.

"When I was a production manager in the South, I contracted for the drilling of all the wells. One of the contractors walked in at Christmas time and put an envelope on my desk and said, "Here's a Christmas present.' There was cash in it. I said, 'Thank you, but this just isn't part of the game.' It wasn't a bribe; it was a gift—but to me it was wrong. I was dealing with a man who understood, but I would have had to return it even if he had been offended. There wasn't much point in taking the money and putting it in petty cash, that wouldn't have solved anything. I don't know how many people face up to these situations—but everybody has the opportunity."

Chapter EIGHT

The Man and the Computer

At his level of management, the young executive has no fear that he will someday have to surrender his power of decision to a computer. For the kind of decisions he makes, the human brain is irreplaceable. The computer's whir (so he believes) can never substitute for thought that is independent—of wires and switches as well as emotions and prejudgments. Generally, the young executive looks on the computer as a means for getting more information, for introducing him to unexplored depths of his business, for opening new doors of discovery— and, of course, for providing him with new reasons to work harder then ever. He brushes aside the thought that he will come into his office some Monday morning and find a computer, squatting and expressionless, behind his desk. He believes that the computer will broaden his managerial scope and so elaborate, rather than simplify, his managerial tasks.

Psychologically structured as he is, the young executive finds inadmissible the thought that his work could ever become easier. When he approaches the computer, therefore, he inevitably looks upon it as a means by which he can extend his managerial authority, and so make his involvement in his job deeper and more inclusive. The experience of young executives who work with computers—or rather, who have computers working for them—bears out this conviction that all computers do for managers is bring them new responsibilities, new problems, and new opportunities. "The computer is a tool, like a soldering iron," says one of them. "It can be a tremendous aid, like PERT techniques for scheduling, or experiments in an engineering laboratory that otherwise would have to be done by trial and error. But I can't see the computer ever replacing management. You have to tell the computer what to do, and you have to organize your problem. You have to think about what everyone does in order to be able to put each piece in the computer. Managers will have to be more skilled in putting operations on a computer, and in weighing data that they didn't have before. But this worry about how the computer is going to take over the world amuses me—all you have to do is pull out the plug."

So the computer simply adds some acceleration to the young executive's drive. "The computer forces me to examine things that I might overlook otherwise," says one of them. Their personal responsibility is not diminished: a young engineer for Kennecott Copper who is working out extensive changes in the traditional patterns of mining ore and calculating their possible effects on a computer says flatly, "If this program doesn't work it will be my fault, not the computer's." Indeed, some executives, like one controller whom we shall name Adams, have been plunged into delicate managerial tasks that would never have come along at all if computers didn't exist.

Adams' problems began with studies of the separate accounting activities, separate statistical departments, and separate data processing activities carried on by the various subsidiaries of his company. The studies soon led Adams and his boss to the conclusion that these separate services should be sawed off from the individual affiliates and grafted together in one centralized office. "At first," recalls Adams, "we couldn't get this plan off the ground. We ran into management prerogatives, and some built-in feeling against change." But Adams' opportunity came when he and his boss made a presentation to his company's chief executive, on costs of the operation of some subsidiaries around New York. "In our review," says Adams, "we pointed out that the number of clerical and nonprofessional employees had gone down since 1960, but that there had been a tremendous increase in managerial and professional people. We found there were lots of reasons: as we told the chief executive and the board, 'You fellows have authorized new activities. You decided that we needed to break out a couple of departments and make a separate business out of it. You broke up one subsidiary into several companies. The number of our plants in Europe has doubled. You created a new layer of management near the top. All this has made our business more complex. We added more people in analysis and planning. We don't question all those decisions to start new organizations and so on. But we say that they are the reason for the increases in managerial employees.' "

Adams continues: "Then we went on to tell the board that in our opinion there was lots of duplication in analysis and planning staffs in the subsidiaries. Each company was building its own staff. They hire professional people, and then they put them on data collection and manipulation and not on real analysis. Half the people on those staffs aren't really analyzing. The companies are using the same data—for different purposes, but the same data. Partly on the basis of our presentation, the chief executive inaugurated a cost-reduction plan. He asked each subsidiary to review the work it was doing, and to tell us, if asked to cut costs 5 percent or 10 percent, what it would cut out. Everybody came up with estimates, saying in effect, 'If the pressure is on us, here is what we can do.' " And, as Adams expected, "Lots of the cuts were in planning and analysis."

At that point the managerial job became especially delicate. Adams and his boss were certain that an integrated computer system, bringing together under one roof the various services being performed by the individual affiliates, would achieve the savings without reduction of—and probably with an increase in, although they didn't promise that—the speed and efficiency for each company of its separate procedures. And the pressures for cost reduction from the chief executive "gave us a golden opportunity," as Adams says, "to implement and accelerate this consolidation." But the plan for consolidation was specifically approved by the boss "only on the condition that we could sell it to the managements of the subsidiaries." That meant that the change had to be made through persuasion, or not at all.

So Adams, who never had a tremor about the wisdom of the plan to integrate, began to work with the managements of the subsidiaries to show them what the change could do. "In one case," he recalls, "there was little resistance. They saw that if we took this staff off their hands, their controller could devote full time to cost analysis, rather than being burdened with this clerical group. They were wholeheartedly for it."

But not every company was so amenable to change. To bring around one recalcitrant subsidiary, Adams began to work very closely with members of its management—proceeding, in a manner habitual to the young executives, with the collection of data, the analysis of it, and the dispassionate and level view of what the analysis indicated and where it led. "We asked this subsidiary," says Adams, "to participate in a study of possible savings in accounting and in the statistical area. Assistant controllers from the company soon came up with reports that we could save this much from elimination of duplication of supervisory people, this much from an integrated computer system, and so on." Armed with that data, Adams began to work his way up through the ranks of the subsidiary, persuading and consolidating support for his views as they went. "We went step by step through the hierarchy, first to the assistant controller, then to the controller, and then to the financial man. Finally we went to the subsidiary's board of directors." With his boss by his side, Adams himself made the presentation—and when it was over, he felt personally gratified by its success, by the achievement of the goal he had set for himself in the first place. "I was especially pleased by this board presentation," he says. "I was more keyed up mentally than I was with the other company. I really felt better coming out of the company where we had problems than I did with the other one."

During all this, Adams also had developed another, even broader plan for functional integration. But he could not push that one to a successful conclusion. "My idea," he says, "was to take all the pension, annuity, and employee savings accounts for all the subsidiaries and put them down in another state, where one big subsidiary company is now doing that work for its own employees. I thought we might save $200,-000 a year that way." But Adams found he could not convince the chief executive of the wisdom of effecting that saving now. "My recommendation was turned down," Adams recalls calmly. "In principle the chief executive agreed with me, but he felt that at the moment there were considerations other than the cost reduction that were more pressing. Those considerations involved people and relationships"—an area that continues to elude computer programming. Adams was somewhat disappointed at not being able to press ahead with his proposal, but taking a disinterested look at the situation—and characteristically refusing to become emotionally involved with the idea simply because it was his own—Adams admitted that he had to agree with the boss: "If I had to make his decision right now, I would decide the same way he did." That does not mean, however, that nothing will ever come of Adams' plan: "I may go back with it when conditions change," he says.

Adams was something less than enthusiastic when he first heard about his assignment to his present job. "I thought, 'Boy, I'm sure taking a step backward. This is routine accounting machine work.'" But he was barely getting started on the assignment when the project for integration of accounting services began, and immediately the change washed away any routine aspects that the job appeared to have. "The thing that has given me incentive here is this project," he says. "I've had more fun than I expected, and I will continue to have." Once the project is over, Adams frankly expects that the job will lose a good deal of its stimulus for him: "Once we get it shaken down and operating smoothly, it won't be much of an attraction for me." But by that time he expects another move: "If I've done the kind of job I want to do, I won't have to speak to management about getting another assignment. They'll know that this job is done from the reports, and from the reduction in static from the other companies." Interestingly enough, however, Adams does not expect that the man who succeeds him in his present job will find it routine or stifling. Instead, a new man will do something new with it: "The man who replaces me won't root the whole thing up, I hope. But he'll probably say something like, 'You did a good job, but you didn't give enough attention to employee relations,' or some other aspect. He'll go to work on that. And he'll find the job fascinating."

Chapter NINE

The Man and the
Sea Around Him

Organizations are abstractions. They ought not to be awarded the traits and the characteristics that really belong not to the organization, but to its individual members. The upper bourgeoisie, Toynbee once wrote, never had a thought or felt an emotion; neither has a business organization.

Dissent from the organization's ways, therefore, is likely to present itself, in the concrete manifestations of real life, as an argument with the boss. The figure of the boss, as psychiatrists have made overwhelmingly clear in recent years, is the father figure—the figure of male authority, which can stir up unresolved fears and anxieties in the breast of the beholder. To face the boss can be a real emotional trauma for some people.

For the young executive, the boss is part of the business problem. And he is an especially difficult part. To determine how to conduct himself when it comes to direct dealings with the boss summons up every ounce of the young man's managerial judgment. One man says he will always have trouble deciding "how hard to fight, how much to rein in emotion. Sometimes your boss expects you to talk back. When he says, 'Stop, I've had enough,' should you really stop? Or does he expect you to bring it up again?" For this man there is no formula: he weighs each situation on its own merits, deciding "how hard to fight" in accordance with the depth of his own conviction. Nor, looking back, is he always sure he was right.

Many young executives jockey to find the right time and the right moment to oppose the boss. One man who works for a brilliant but domineering chief executive reports, "I learned to pick the right time to tell Jack what I think. I found he couldn't stand criticism in front of a group. So now I wait till we're alone—I can get results by telling him anything I want then." Another manager who works for a many-layered electronics company says frankly, "I had worked for Tom once before and didn't like it much. But now I find he's matured, and so have I. We can communicate. He gets some ideas that aren't worth a damn; they're horrifying. Sometimes I tell him so on the spot, sometimes I say I'll go home and think about it. Then I work up my case, and he usually goes along with it."

Still another manager—in this case, one who is totally engrossed in his work—recalls how he responded to what he considered undue interference with the way he was running his division. Late one afternoon this man found out that the amount of money that his division was to contribute to corporate research was being determined by the chief of the company's research organization. Not without a trace of grim pleasure, he says, "I blew my stack. I called a meeting that started at ten o'clock that night. At three in the morning I called the research chief, woke him up and told him, 'The hell with that research budget of yours. We're not going to put in a nickel.'

"The next morning the company president called me into his office. I held out my hand and said, 'Go ahead, rap my knuckles. But nobody can spend my division's money without my approval. If they can, then you can't hold me responsible for the p. and l.' He admitted I was right, but he said, 'You might have been a little more diplomatic with Peter.' I guess I might have—but I sure got results fast." Thus, in business situations, the young executive speaks out forcefully for what he believes in. His own broad business knowledge, and his own factual grasp of individual problems, support him in that forcefulness.

In his own eagerness, the boss can sometimes push too hard. When that happens, he is not likely to gain much if the man he is pushing is an aggressive young executive, who usually won't suffer pushing gladly—primarily because he is already driving himself, for his own reasons, about as hard as a man can. One young executive, hounded by an overzealous boss, looked within himself, and found himself capable of a virtuoso performance like this one: "The boss looked like an s.o.b. to me, and I worse to him, at first. He bugged me about so many little details—like the landscaping around the plant, for God's sake, I couldn't have cared less, but to answer his questions I had to look into the whole thing myself. It turned out there was good reason for everything that had been done, but I really didn't want to get into it at all. Finally the situation got so bad that I actually started looking around for another job. I didn't make any secret of that, but I didn't threaten anybody with it. You can't blackmail this company. If I had decided to leave, I would have called my boss and asked, 'Do you want me to go now, or wait a little while?' But I decided not to leave. Instead I hit on a formula for handling this man: I started treating him exactly the way he was treating me. I began to tell him exactly what I thought. When he bothered me too much, I said, 'Stop it, you're bothering me.' So he stopped. Now we get along.

"He still doesn't exactly think I'm a hero. But if he did, how long could that last? That flush of pleasure can't stay on his face forever. He's got his problems too. Next time you look, his face is gray and he's asking, 'What have you done for me lately?' I had some cliff-hangers last year. Our business is seasonal, and we lay out money in the first three months but don't see the profits back until the very end of the second quarter. We were into the first week of June before it broke. Then suddenly it got great and we were shipping that crap out of the warehouse like popcorn. We shipped until midnight of June 30th and we did very well, far better than we ever expected. The boss had been worried and calling every day and the finish was pretty thrilling. On Friday he called to congratulate me. He really was very flattering, and I felt fine about the whole thing. Then he called again early on Monday morning to complain. He said, 'Your receivables are way too high.' Hell, we had just finished shipping it out. So who's a hero?"

Exactly how the boss reacts to these attitudes and expressions must go largely unrecorded. One opinion on the subject, however, comes from the head of an executive-search firm that seeks to supply presidents or successors to presidents to companies in need. Says this man: "Should a man get along with his boss? That's the toughest question in business today. It comes down to what the boss is looking for—is he really looking for somebody he wants as a replacement. One executive said to me, 'We've got all the techniques of finding the right guy and of measuring his performance. We've got all the right people in the right places. But we don't know where our next president is coming from.' When they look for somebody, they like a guy who has all the rough edges knocked off; who has got lots of zip but not too much; who is aggressive and ambitious, but watches his P's and Q's while he's at it. We have all the means of getting people where they belong, but when you look for that special fire that makes a president— well, we just don't have any way of finding it. I guess you could say that you have to prostitute your principles everywhere—so the question is, does 'getting along with the boss' mean doing the job, or being a yes man? About all we can conclude is that the presidents we know are not the hounds that ran with the pack.

"What these young managers complain about most is not being given enough responsibility. Fundamentally, they all want to run something. They have, by and large, matured beyond the concept of 'all that dead wood in the way.' The dead wood may be there, various organizational obstacles may be there. But these men are beyond the idea of 'Why doesn't somebody sweep it all out of the way?' For them, the idea is how to get around the situation. They're not in basic training —they're full-fledged qualified troopers facing a field problem. So they attack the problem."

Whatever deep conclusions can be drawn from this capacity of the young executive dispassionately to face the father figure must be left to the psychiatrists. The notable part of the capacity, for our purposes, is the objectivity it entails—the disinterested quality that the young executive introduces into his relationships with the boss. He constantly analyzes that relationship, seeks to weigh it, to keep it in balance, to decide when it remains within tolerable limits, and when it becomes intolerable. But he is remarkably impersonal about the whole problem—sometimes he succeeds in pushing it away from him, and looking upon drama and players as though he were not on stage at all. He appears to be able to suppress, or perhaps he does not experience, the emotional overtones that a meeting with the boss—Big Daddy—can contain for other people. But in the formal realtionships with his superiors that fall outside of the detailed discussion of business problems, the young executive must often pay proper respect to ceremony. If he is based in the provinces, he spends more time than he likes in meeting airplanes and attending social affairs. He entertains company brass a good deal, and the weight of protocol can become heavy and tedious. Especially in smaller towns and cities, where he is usually only a transient, he is often involved in some aspects of community life that may not interest him very much. His company—I.B.M. and G.E. are among those conspicuous in this regard—is apt to assess the man's position and conduct in the community as part of his general job performance. So he goes to church, probably, whether or not he is a religious man. And he may join the P.T.A., whether or not he is burning with a desire to improve the community's educational system. To use P.T.A. membership as evidence of a cultural activity on the part of the young executive may therefore not always be fair. Often his membership may result partly at least from a desire to do what the company may expect of him.

Whether those activities constitute conformity, and therefore should be condemned, is a moot point. But one might pause for a moment to consider Sidney Hook's pertinent comments: "I see no specific virtue in the attitude of conformity or non-comformity. The important thing is that it should be voluntary, rooted in considered judgment, an authentic expression of some value or some insight. Before evaluating 'conformity' or 'non-conformity' I should like to know to and with what a person is conforming or not conforming and how. . . . Under the Weimar Republic, Hitler was a non-conformist. Under the Czarist regime, Dostoevsky was a conformist."

In any case, most other kinds of surface conformity by the young executives—notably dress—are simply not relevant to corporate relationships, despite the popular fiction on the subject. A division vice-president of RCA Victor says, "I have yet to see the people described in some of these books. Conformity is not what I've been told is wanted of me. Oh—I suppose you have to be clean." A man from Western Electric asserts: "All that drivel about executives who wear high socks because they don't want to expose their skin—I resent it. It's embarrassing. What difference does that make?" One officer of the Chase Manhattan Bank, denying the charge that all bank executives must wear vests, said quietly: "Why, even David doesn't always wear one." And, presumably, he doesn't care whether anyone else does. The boss doesn't impose too far.

To cope with the boss, however, turns out to be only one part of the young executive's intricate associations with company people. Around him heaves a sea of subordinates that have to be manipulated. To handle them requires just as much care as to handle the boss. When one young man went abroad from headquarters to revamp the operations of a subsidiary oil company, he found that the subsidiary "was doing everything, even collecting the garbage. There was $7,800,000 worth of warehouse stock. They had enough spare parts for the water plant so that if an A-bomb hit it they could repair it on the spot. The shop foreman wouldn't think of running a lathe unless he had a spare motor for it. He had a hundred spare motors for a hundred lathes. I'm not blaming the people there, that's the way they were taught. They had worked for a manager who insisted that they be able to repair anything immediately. It was a matter of teaching them to do what we do in the States, leasing cars and not repairing them yourself, letting contractors run the camps, putting somebody else in the garbage business. Your own employees you keep for your own work. But the resistance was horrible.

"The problem comes when you drive too hard, when you get overzealous and gain those two feet, and aren't willing to fall back a foot before making the next two. You have to buck the tide slowly, and you have to prove your way. Once you've sold yourself to the people who work for you, once they're convinced that you're not building a career on their graves, then you can sit back. Then they'll tell you ways to save money—ways you could never dream of."

Many others show the same kind of consciousness of their techniques in managing the people below them on the ladder. And they also have a cold ability to assess their own skill at this function. Curiously enough, that assessment often leads them to the judgment that, far from suppressing their own views too much, they are sometimes inclined to push too hard and too fast for their own good. "In dealing with others I have a tendency to be overbearing, to project too much of my personality on someone else," confesses a young man from Jersey Standard. "For example, I start talking to somebody and really want to find out his views, but my chances of getting what I want are substantially reduced when I project too much of what I think. Modulation can get you further in certain circumstances." An insurance-company executive sounds a similar note. "I'm less tactful than might be smart at times," he comments. "I don't commit real breaches, but it still makes my job harder. On occasion, when I moved in it might have been better to wait a bit."

Since he works hard himself, the young executive expects hard work from the managers below him. When he takes over a new division, he makes changes where he can, with a view to bringing in people who are cut from the same bolt of cloth that he is. One I.T.T. executive says calmly, "When I came here, I inherited fifteen people. I've got two left. I had to fire or transfer the others; they didn't step up to doing the job the way I wanted it done. When you're trying to increase profits 10 to 15 percent a year, you can't do it with ordinary management. When a problem comes up, I want my man to take action, and take it then. One fellow who worked around here was very able. But he had come to a certain way of living, he wanted to go bowling every Thursday night. I admire the guy, he's just as right as I am. I only say that if he's going to work for me, he can't go bowling every Thursday. He's got to work my way."

While he prefers subordinates who reflect his own image, the young executive recognizes the differences in attitude that age may bring. One man recalls that he put a much older man on his staff because that older man enjoyed the confidence and respect of others in the department. "I took him into my department," the young manager explains, "even though he told me at the time that he didn't want to get involved in a lot of overtime. Then, after he had been on the job for a while, he called me and suggested that we work at night to get a particular project done. I was really glad. He's fifty-five and he's still got the spark. But if a man thirty-three had told me that he didn't want to get involved in a lot of overtime, I would have looked for someone else."

His own fondness for facts is one trait that the young executive is anxious to find mirrored in the people who work for him. He counts on facts in his relations with his superiors, and in much the same spirit he looks for factual evaluation from his subordinates. One assistant treasurer who revamped his company's accounting system at a cost of around $1 million recalls that one year after the new system's installation he asked a man who had assisted him in its preparation to see whether it was doing everything that they had expected of it. "But the man couldn't do it," the assistant treasurer says. "He was psychologically incapable of going around the track and making an appraisal. He could look at the good, but he couldn't look at the bad. Some people need to feel perfect; they can't admit an error. To others of us, it doesn't matter. I had to get the report from somebody else."

One young executive was sent from the headquarters company to take over the operation of a major subsidiary. In the course of a few days, he was able to see many things that his managerial instincts told him were wrong. But he was just as responsive to the instinct that informed him that he could not make all the corrections and improvements himself. "Walking through our plant," he now recalls, "I'd see these cardboard boxes full of rejects. I look again, and I see George Washington's face on every one—they cost us twenty-five cents apiece. We had millions of our consumer products in the field—all obsolete. I asked the sales manager for his sales forecasts and he just looked at me. There were none—just a lot of wheels spinning. I knew nothing was being done well in the plant. Our foreman didn't know how to be a foreman. Decisions were being made in the wrong places, sometimes by the girls on the line—it was costing us a fortune. We had a guy in charge of quality control that I wouldn't let inspect hot dogs. The chain of command was too long. It was an industrial engineer's dream."

The young manager, however, did not step in on the operating level himself. "I didn't want to fire the quality control man. He was too far from me—I just couldn't be sure enough. The manager of manufacturing had to do that. He was a personal friend of mine. He had come from the parent company too. He had been here a year studying details. I had to come to the conclusion that he wasn't doing much of a job. So I followed one of the simplest theories of management I know—put the brightest guys in charge. I gave the management of manufacturing to Tom—he's one of the brightest guys. Now the plant is turned around. The new guy in quality control—he's a tiger. There are still some decisions where we have to roll the bones, sure. But operations are streamlined. We're responsive to new ideas."

Listen to Them Talk

Subordinates can be cajoled, bullied, and even fired. But certainly they have to be coped with—and that can be anguishing.

Of firings and guitars: *"Firing people is one thing that doesn't get any easier with practice. The closer you are to it, the tougher it is. About the only way you can sleep nights is to figure that it's like the army—what you're doing is best for the war. I know it has to be done, but I really get sick when the time comes. I try to keep the business standard in mind first— that's cold and objective. Then I look at the man and let the human standard enter in. I make the most generous settlement that I can, and I keep asking myself: 'Can he feel slighted in any way?' Still, by the time it's over I wish I were playing the guitar for a living instead."*

Of subordinates and bottles: *"An immediate subordinate of mine had too much to drink at one of our dinners. He started heckling my boss right in the middle of a speech. He'd had so much by then he didn't know what he was doing. But I had to break it up right on the spot. After all, it was a company group. Then I got hold of this man a couple of days later and told him off. Either give up the drinking or else. I told my associates and they were amazed that I would talk to a subordinate that way, especially a man older than I. Maybe they felt that at our level you shouldn't have to do that. But we try to make sure that we promote people who deserve to be promoted. And I think we ought to demote guys who should be demoted."*

Of wives and loneliness: *"I've had some success because I've been in the middle of the financial community and in big companies too. I think I know enough about how a banker thinks—and sometimes they can be very naïve about why a company succeeds—and enough about how a big industrialist thinks so that I can make agreements that they will both accept. It's a fascinating area.*

"When I changed jobs recently, I had a terrible time. The new company was really near the brink. I won't go through that again. I think the experience of having had older men work for me helped me a lot, I could use the older people who were emotionally very stable. I'm a great sleeper, but there was a forty-five-day period when I was up pacing most of the night. My wife really couldn't understand it. I was alone. I finally got us a $32 million loan one-half a point over the prime rate—I was surprised to do anything like that well—and that helped to save us. Now I wouldn't give up the experience for all the money in the world. I learned you can get wonderful results with people."

Sometimes the young manager may be sent to operate under an older man, when he and the top management both know that the older man is not doing the job well enough. Here is how one young executive handled that kind of situation:

"Ed knew why I was there—to cut expenses $4 million or $5 million a year. That was my job, and that was what I dug into. There were some nip-and-tuck times: Ed was sixty-three, a tough old do-it-yourself field hand, and he was the kind of man who had never had an assistant. In our company, they never lay it on the line to a man like that and say, 'Look, you're over the hill.' I had to work with him. It annoyed me at times. But in the end we had a mutual respect, and a good relationship. It worked out because I decided it behooves the younger man to accommodate himself in some ways. I worked overtime at that. And I finally came to the conclusion that it was worth it—you can learn a lot from these old-timers."

Another young executive in television recalls with wry amusement how he scotched a colleague's creative impulse: *"We were going to televise the Surgeon General's report on smoking. It bore down pretty hard on smoking as a cause of cancer. Then I had a call from one of our really good salesmen—he had this idea, and he called in great excitement. He wanted to approach a cigarette company and try to talk them into sponsoring the televising of the report. I said, 'Look, you're a little tired.' He insisted. Then I said, 'Look, Tom, great idea, very creative. But the answer is no.' What the guy hadn't figured, of course, was that even if the cigarette company hadn't thrown him out, their sponsorship would have compromised the objectivity of the report. We put the program on without a sponsor, even though we hated to let such programs go unsponsored. We like to show there's support for programs in this category."*

Chapter TEN

The Cocoon that
Surrounded Him

The portrait of the young executive has been drawn mainly from long sittings with him—interviews which were extensive in length, and remarkable in frankness. They were by far the single most revealing source of information about the man's character. As the period of research that preceded *Fortune*'s first article on the young executive came to an end, it was fascinating to watch the similarities in outlook emerge in the talks with man after man. At first glance it would seem impossible that this one, too—fat where the other was lean, balding where the other had looked so young, exceptionally dapper perhaps where most of the others had given their dress only the minimal amount of thought it required—could echo the same, familiar thoughts and feelings. But inevitably he did: as he warmed to the discussion, his attitudes, his ample confidence, the carapace he wore came clear, and the resemblances, in the end, came to be easily recognizable. In the last interviews, one could predict what some of the man's responses would be—always a sign, indeed, that the period of research is ending.

The man's own words, which have been given here in generous measure, testify to the veracity of the portrait. Another testimonial comes in the form of letters which came to *Fortune,* a magazine not widely read by women, from wives who recognized their husbands from this likeness. Several of the letters were positively effusive in style; some ended with a sigh, or on a "I guess we both understand that there isn't anything *anybody* can do about Charlie" kind of note. One young wife telephoned to announce, with a good bit of humor and just a tang of annoyance, that she thought she might sue *Fortune:* everybody in the neighborhood, she said, knew we were talking about her husband, and she didn't especially like the kind of person that we made him out to be. But she recognized him from the description, too, and she had to agree that it was Charlie, all right.

An especially striking letter came from a young woman in upstate New York. Referring to the opening article in *Fortune*'s series, she said, "There were so many quotes that I have actually heard from my husband that it is just as if I were listening to him expound on his favorite subject. . . . The sentence 'His security lies within himself' has been his creed, his motto, his way of life, almost to the point of revulsion toward people who seek 'security' from their employment. Work preoccupies all his waking, and often some of his sleeping hours."

To supplement the personal interviews, and to ascertain how wide the support was for the conclusions that they led to, a questionnaire about the young executives was drawn up and sent out under *Fortune* auspices. One should state, with considerable emphasis, that the purpose of the questionnaire was only to seek some corroboration to what was essentially an interpretive journalistic inquiry. Neither questionnaire nor inquiry was intended to lead to a sociological study, although that is, partly at least, what we ended up with.

The questionnaire went to 150 companies on *Fortune*'s list of the 500 largest industrial corporations, and to 50 of the country's largest banks, insurance, and merchandising companies. At *Fortune*'s request, officers in these companies forwarded the questionnaires to men in the company ranks who met *Fortune*'s definition of age (thirty to forty-five) and position (somewhere in the upper levels, as described in Chapter One). The companies were asked to choose *successful* company men. Some 4,000 questionnaires were sent out, and tabulations were made by Erdos & Morgan from 1,003 questionnaires selected at random from the total replies received.

All replies were confidential. They were returned to *Fortune* directly, not through the offices of the company. They were unsigned, and the company's name was not included anywhere on the replies.

The entire questionnaire is reprinted as an appendix on page 179.

Here is what the answers to the questionnaires revealed.

Age. The average age of the respondents was 39.5 years. The largest single group (11.5 percent of the total who replied) was born in 1921, followed by 1922 (9.5 percent), and then 1919 (8.4 percent). Very few of the respondents were born in 1930 or after.

Marital Status. Overwhelmingly, the men who answered were married: 96.8 percent. And, interestingly, they just as overwhelmingly tend to stay married: only 1 percent of them have been divorced, and, of that 1 percent, all but .05 percent have remarried. No member of the group had been divorced twice. One might conclude that this young executive, who burns himself up in his business, also manages to keep the fires going at home pretty well: that 1 percent divorce rate is much below the national average. And one may assume from the high rate of remarriage that the young executive, while he doesn't mind being alone in his business judgments, wants a companion at home to answer the door when he returns—late —from the office.

As other replies reveal (see below) the young executive is very well educated. But his wife is not, at least not to the same degree. Over half of the wives (52.3 percent) do not have college degrees. That happier home life may result in part at least from the fact that the hard-driving, hard-competing young executive, when he finally gets home, is easily the intellectual superior there.

His children. Again, an overwhelming number of the respondents who are married have children (99.4 percent). As though to demonstrate his objectivity, the young executive has managed to father exactly the same number of boys as girls: on the average, he has 1.4 boys, and 1.4 girls, thus enlivening his life with whatever joys 2.8 children, playing around the house, can bring a man. Of the children who are of educable age, 22.7 percent go to private school; the number in private colleges, however, goes down to 7.6 percent of the college attendants.

His own education. Only 3 percent of the respondents ended their education in high school; 9.6 percent attended college, but did not get a degree. All the rest who answered the question have college degrees. Exactly half of them went on to take postgraduate degrees. More of the young executives attended private college, for whatever reason, than are sending their children there: 20.5 percent went to Ivy League colleges, and 43.5 percent to private colleges outside of the Ivy League. The balance attended public universities.

Among fields of study, business and engineering took most of the young executive's attention; 28.9 percent studied engineering, of which 8.3 percent concentrated on mechanical engineering, and 6.9 percent on electrical. Almost as many as studied engineering took business study while still undergraduates: 28.2 percent were business majors, of whom 14.9 percent studied business administration in preparation for their careers as managers. Accounting and finance took the major attention of another 8.7 percent of the students of business, and the balance scattered elsewhere through the business field. After engineering and business came social science, which was studied by 20.6 percent of the total; by far the majority of the social scientists studied economics. After the social sciences came the physical sciences: 11.7 percent of the group made their undergraduate effort there, mostly in chemistry. Ranking fifth in undergraduate fields of study came the humanities: 10.9 percent majored there. The rest of the college graduates divided their attention between mathematics (4 percent of the total(and other professions outside of engineering (1.5 percent are lawyers), and a collection of miscellaneous studies.

Clearly, they wanted their education badly enough to work for it. Almost exactly one man in three (33.6 percent) attended night school, working, as a rule, either for a Master of Business Administration or a Master of Science. And fully 80 percent of all the college graduates contributed something to the cost of their own education. Of that number, 35 percent earned more than half the cost of their education, and 31.6 percent earned about half; the rest contributed "a small amount." They seem to have done quite well scholastically, at least if holding a scholarship is any indication of scholastic achievement: 30.2 percent held scholarships. Over 25 percent graduated with some kind of academic honors.

Looking back to their formal schooling, 71 percent of the men who replied indicated that they would choose the same field of study. Twenty-six percent, however, would change the past if they could, and would change it, it seems, to put more emphasis on the professions. Of that dissatisfied 26 percent, 36 percent would go into a profession, most favoring the law. And 28 percent of the same group would study business, most favoring business administration. Engineering and the humanities are the next most popular fields among the men who decided that their formal preparation for business and for life could have been better.

The reasons why these men would like the chance to change their educational background, if they could, are complicated. Among those who said "No" to the question "If you could start your formal schooling over again, would you choose the same field of study?" these reasons were given:

A DIFFERENT FIELD WOULD OFFER:	%
Better advancement, more money, earning power, more opportunity, compensation, better hours and benefits, etc.	13.7
More broadening, creative, intellectual; applicable to various industries better educational background, etc.	18.6
I like it more, more interested in it, personal satisfaction, more suited to it, greater challenge	29.7
Service to society, enables you to encourage and inspire people	5.3
Bright new field, increasing interest in field	1.9
Closer to my job needs, to my profession	26.2
Prospect of self-employment independence	4.9

Fully 26.2 percent would exchange their educational background, if they could, for one closer to their "job needs"—a further indication of what the personnel men call the "job orientation" of young executives.

His life today. The young executive generally occupies a single-family house: 93.1 percent of the respondents live in houses, while only 6.4 percent live in apartments. The average market value of his house is $36,907. Breakdowns are given below:

	%
Less than $20,000	8.8
$20,000 to 24,999	11.3
25,000 to 29,999	13.7
30,000 to 34,999	14.1

35,000 to 39,999	12.5
40,000 to 44,999	11.5
45,000 to 49,999	5.8
50,000 to 59,999	9.5
60,000 to 69,999	5.4
70,000 to 99,999	3.1
100,000 and over	1.1

When the house was built:

YEAR	%
Before 1930	10.7
1930-1939	8.8
1940-1949	8.2
1950-1954	14.1
1955	5.4
1956	5.7
1957	6.0
1958	5.7
1959	8.0
1960	6.5
1961	7.0
1962	5.7
1963-1964	6.0
Not stated whether own house	2.2

There followed a series of questions about other material aspects of the young executive's life. Replies indicated that these men live on a comfortable but not elaborate level. More of them have two cars in their immediate family than have only one:

HOW MANY CARS DO YOU AND YOUR IMMEDIATE FAMILY NOW OWN?	%
One	40.2
Two	55.0
Three	3.1
Four	0.2
None	1.5
No answer	—

But most of the cars are low-priced; there are few privately owned Cadillacs.

In compiling results of the questionnaires, no more than three cars were taken, even when respondents indicated ownership of more than three cars.

U.S. MAKES	%
Buick	7.2
" Special ('61-'64)	0.1
" Riviera ('63-'64)	0.1
Cadillac	1.6
Chevrolet (Impala)	16.6
" Chevy II ('62-'64)	0.6
" Chevelle ('64)	0.1
" Corvair (Monza, Lakewood)	2.6
" Corvette (Stingray)	0.2
Chrysler (Newport)	1.5
" Imperial	0.2
Dodge (except Dart) (Lancer)	3.1
" Dart	0.1
Ford	17.5
" Falcon	2.1
" Fairlane ('62-'64)	0.1
" Thunderbird	2.4
Lincoln	0.2
" Continental	0.1
Mercury (except Comet) (Meteor)	2.4
" Comet	1.2
Oldsmobile	7.5
" F85 ('61-'64)	0.6
Plymouth	5.0
" Valiant	1.1
Pontiac (Grand Prix)	7.5
" Tempest, LeMans	0.9
Rambler (Classic, Ambassador, Nash)	4.5
Rambler American	0.2
Studebaker (Avanti)	0.6
" Lark	0.3
Willys (Jeepster)	0.1
Misc. U.S. Cars	0.6

FOREIGN MAKES	%
Hillman (Minx)	0.7
Jaguar	0.4
MG (Magnette, MGA)	0.6

FOREIGN MAKES	%
Mercedes-Benz	0.7
Renault (Caravelle, Dauphine)	1.1
Volkswagen (Karmann Ghia)	4.4
Austin-Healey	0.4
Misc. Foreign Cars	2.1
Make not specified	0.2

YEAR OF MODEL	%
1964	5.1
1963	20.6
1962	18.2
1961	13.3
1960	13.6
1959	9.3
1958	4.1
1957	3.9
1956	3.1
1955	3.7
1954 or earlier	4.7
No answer	0.4

BOUGHT	%
New	75.0
Used	24.4
No answer	0.6

His leisure hours. The young executive, it appears, is both a sportsman and a reader. His favorite spectator sport is football, which 78.9 percent of these men regularly enjoy; baseball, the national game, runs a clear second, with 46.7 percent listing it as a source of regular enjoyment. As for participating in sports, he does a good deal of that, too: one man in three belongs to a country club. The overwhelming favorite game to participate in is golf, selected by 53.4 percent; swimming, tennis, fishing, and hunting follow.

The tables:

AS A SPECTATOR:	%
Football	78.9
Baseball, softball	46.7

As a Spectator:	%
Basketball	22.2
Golf	13.4
Ice hockey	12.2
Tennis	2.8
Track & field	3.4
All other spectator sports	6.6
None (specified)	6.3
No answer	8.8

As a Participant:	%
Swimming	25.4
Baseball, softball	4.5
Basketball	3.6
Golf	53.4
Misc. other ball games (football, volleyball, etc.)	3.5
Tennis, squash	21.2
Track & field	0.3
Skiing	11.3
Fishing	16.8
Sailing & boating	11.6
Bowling	13.7
Hunting & shooting	12.2
Ice skating	4.4
Camping, hiking	4.8
Ping-pong	2.4
Flying	1.0
Horse riding	1.4
Water skiing	2.7
Handball	2.2
Misc. others	4.4
None (specified)	6.3
No answer	3.2

As for hobbies, 31.3 percent of these educated men claimed "reading" first. Gardening followed (16.1 percent) and then came music and photography. The tables:

What Are Your Hobbies?	%
Reading	31.3
Gardening	16.1
Music—hi-fi, TV, radio	13.0

WHAT ARE YOUR HOBBIES?	%
Photography	10.8
Woodworking, carpentry	10.4
All other arts & crafts (model making, metalworking, etc.) & unspec.	3.2
Cards, bridge, etc.	9.7
Cooking	1.9
Travel	3.1
Painting	2.3
Instrument playing	2.8
Theater	0.9
Civic work	5.1
Politics	1.5
Church work	0.8
Amateur radio, electronics	2.4
"Do-it-yourself"	2.1
Collecting (stamp, art, fish, guns, etc.)	6.1
Misc. others (writing, astronomy, nature, etc.)	12.7
None	4.0
No answer	17.0

The questionnaire then moved in to take a closer look at those reading habits. The men are readers, all right, having read in the twelve-month period before receipt of the questionnaire 10.9 books, on an average. The breakdowns:

ABOUT HOW MANY BOOKS, UNRELATED TO YOUR BUSINESS, HAVE YOU READ IN THE PAST YEAR?	%
1	3.5
2	9.2
3	8.2
4	6.5
5	7.0
6	8.2
7	1.7
8	2.7
9	1.0
10	7.5
11-14	9.5
15-19	6.4

ABOUT HOW MANY BOOKS, UNRE- LATED TO YOUR BUSINESS, HAVE YOU READ IN THE PAST YEAR?	%
20-24	5.5
25-49	7.5
50 or more	3.7
Indefinite	1.2
None	8.2
No answer	2.5

Their taste in the selection of books, however, doesn't appear to be the most highly cultivated:

IF YOU CAN RECALL ANY OF THE TITLES, PLEASE LIST A FEW:	%
Seven Days in May	10.3
Fail-safe	8.4
James Bond (Books by Ian Fleming, except *Dr. No*)	6.6
Advise and Consent	5.9
The Guns of August	5.6
The Rise and Fall of the Third Reich	5.6
My Life in Court	4.7
The Making of the President 1960	4.4
The Prize	4.4
The Agony and the Ecstasy	3.9
The Shoes of the Fisherman	3.6
To Kill a Mockingbird	3.2
Profiles in Courage	2.9
Uhuru	2.8
Youngblood Hawke	2.1
The Rothschilds	2.1
The Group	2.0
Lord of the Flies	2.0
The Devil's Advocate	1.8
Dr. No	1.2
The Affluent Society	0.6
Misc. others	66.7
No answer	24.4

Business reading, too, took much of their leisure time and attention:

ABOUT HOW MANY BOOKS, RELATED TO YOUR BUSINESS, HAVE YOU READ IN THE PAST YEAR?	%
1	8.0
2	12.0
3	10.4
4	5.8
5	6.9
6	5.6
7	1.2
8	1.2
9	0.6
10	4.6
11-14	3.4
15 or more	4.2
Indefinite	2.4
None	25.4
No answer	8.3

SUBJECT MATTER	%
Human side, people	47.5
Technical—concerning products, etc.	35.2
Unidentified	2.6
No answer	34.1

IS THERE A DIFFERENCE BETWEEN THE READING YOU DO IN YOUR OFFICE AND THE READING YOU DO AT HOME?	%
Yes, I read completely different material	58.2
No, my home reading is usually directly or indirectly related to my office work	30.6
Both, some of each	9.1
No answer	2.1

And the magazines get their share:

PLEASE LIST THE MAGAZINES OF ALL KINDS WHICH YOU READ REGULARLY:	%
Time	50.6
Life	47.2

PLEASE LIST THE MAGAZINES OF ALL KINDS WHICH YOU READ REGULARLY:	%
Business Week	33.7
Fortune	31.9
Reader's Digest	20.9
Newsweek	18.4
Saturday Evening Post	17.7
Look	14.6
Sports Illustrated	14.4
Harvard Business Review	14.0
U.S. News & World Report	14.0
National Geographic	12.4
Forbes	11.5
New Yorker	11.4
Nation's Business	7.6
Playboy	5.5
Better Homes & Gardens	4.4
Chemical Week	4.1
Saturday Review	4.1
Holiday	4.0
Changing Times	3.7
Harper's	3.4
Dun's Review	3.2
Sales Management	3.0
True	3.0
Chemical and Engineering News	2.8
Sunset	2.6
National Underwriter	2.3
Business Management	2.0
McCall's	1.8
Misc. others	62.3
None (specified)	1.1
No answer	1.7

About his work.   America is an open society. The vision of its classlessness is not a dream or a mirage. De Tocqueville was early in his perception of mobility as a feature of American society, and the point has been made by social observers many times since. Today, it seems as valid, or perhaps more valid than it ever was. In his book *Occupational Mobility*, Lloyd Warner shows that movement from the factory into middle management was still taking place: "In spite of the pessimistic predictions about an immobilized society," Warner concludes, "the evidence shows that our society is more flexible than it was."

The young executives have demonstrated the truth of, and capitalized on, the continuing mobility of American life. Almost half of them (49.8 percent) began their business careers in the lower ranks of management, from which they have climbed to the upper ranks. But, surprisingly, a large number of them—16.7 percent—began as laborers semiskilled, or skilled workers. Far more started in business at those low economic levels than started close to the top: only 2 percent began their careers in the middle ranks of management, and only .2 percent began "at the top," presumably as a result of father's or father-in-law's position. Here is the way they answered the question "At what level did you begin your business career?":

AT WHAT LEVEL DID YOU BEGIN YOUR BUSINESS CAREER?	%
Laborer	3.7
Semiskilled worker	6.0
Skilled worker	7.0
Lower ranks of management	49.8
Middle ranks of management	2.0
At the top	0.2

OTHER	%
Salesman, salesman trainee	6.7
Engineer, jr. engineer	4.0
All other professional and technical	7.1
Clerical	6.9
Misc. others	6.1
No answer	0.5

Their mobility, too, is evidenced by the way they have moved freely through the business world in the course of their lives. On an average, they have been with the company that now employs them for 11.1 years; 14.2 percent have been with their present company from fifteen to sixteen years, and 12.4 from seventeen to nineteen years—in both cases, that stretch of time probably covers the full span of the man's mature working life. But, unexpectedly, substantial numbers of them have been rolling around pretty freely: 8.4 percent have been with their present company two years or less, and 8 percent from three to four years. In total, 25 percent of them have been with their present employer for six years or less—a high percentage. The particulars:

How Long Have You Been with Your Present Company?	%
2 years or less	8.4
3-4 years	8.0
5-6 "	8.6
7-8 "	9.4
9-10 "	11.4
11-12 "	9.4
13-14 "	11.7
15-16 "	14.2
17-19 "	12.4
20 years or more	6.2
No answer	0.3

Among them, 37.8 percent have remained with the company they started out with—a high percentage. But 62 percent have changed jobs at least once. And many have changed two, three, and four times. Among those who have worked for more than one company, the average number of moves is two. The breakdown:

Have You Worked for Companies Other than Your Present Company?	%
Yes	62.0
No	37.8
No answer	0.2

If "Yes," for How Many Years in Total?	%
1 year or less	13.2
2 years	12.3
3 "	8.4
4 "	8.8
5 "	8.7
6 "	6.6
7 "	5.0
8 "	5.0

IF "YES," FOR HOW MANY YEARS IN TOTAL?	%
9 "	2.1
10 "	5.1
11-14 years	11.7
15-19 "	8.4
20 years or more	3.4
No answer	1.3

IF "YES," HOW MANY TIMES HAVE YOU MOVED FROM ONE COMPANY TO ANOTHER IN YOUR ADULT BUSINESS LIFE?	%
One	48.2
Two	23.2
Three	15.9
Four	5.6
Five	3.4
Six	1.0
Seven	—
Eight	0.2
Nine	—
Ten	0.2
No answer	2.2

Like the reasons why many of them wish they had a different kind of education, the reasons why they have changed jobs are complex. Many of them are implied in other parts of this book, where gratifications and motivations are discussed. The tabulation of their motives in changing jobs reveals very vividly the emphasis they put on "an opportunity to get ahead."

WHICH OF THE FOLLOWING CONSIDERATIONS WERE MOST IMPORTANT TO YOU WHEN YOU MADE A MOVE?	%
I was blocked on my old job, and saw an opportunity to move ahead faster somewhere else	42.3
I moved because I got more money immediately, as well as a more promising future	48.6
My old situation was pretty intolerable, and I wanted a change	15.4
I felt I had a couple of strikes against	

WHICH OF THE FOLLOWING CONSIDER-ATIONS WERE MOST IMPORTANT TO YOU WHEN YOU MADE A MOVE?	%
me on my record in my old job, and I wanted a fresh start	0.8
No answer	14.8

The source of satisfaction, of course, comes from "the sense of accomplishment." Only 7.2 percent of those answering the question "What is the greatest single source of satisfaction to you on your present job?" replied, "The fact that it pays very well." And, interestingly, only 8.6 percent identified the imposition of uniformity as a source of dissatisfaction:

WHAT IS THE GREATEST SINGLE SOURCE OF SATISFACTION TO YOU ON YOUR PRESENT JOB?	%
The sense of accomplishment I get from it	44.0
The fact that it pays very well	7.2
The belief that if I perform well, I've got a good future here	27.7
I have some real creative opportunities right now, as well as promise for the future	40.2
The knowledge that if I perform ably, I am secure in my tenure, and should have a decent retirement	3.7
No answer	0.4

WHAT IS THE GREATEST SOURCE OF DIS-SATISFACTION?	%
The company is too big, and I never get a real sense of accomplishment as a result of my own performance	8.3
I don't make enough money to get myself and my family the things we want	21.1
Uniformity is imposed, and I never really get a chance to express my individual, dissenting beliefs	8.6
The company thinks the group or committee have to be harmonious around	

WHAT IS THE GREATEST SOURCE OF DIS-SATISFACTION?	%
here, and I secretly hate harmony	4.7
None applicable	27.1
No answer	31.0

Generally, they began their careers at a level higher than their fathers achieved. Where 16.7 percent of the young executives began at the three lowest levels of business, 20.2 percent of their fathers ended up there. But the sons, of course, are far better educated than the parents were: only 26.6 percent of the fathers, and only 19.6 percent of the mothers, were college graduates. The breakdowns:

WAS YOUR FATHER . . .	%
A laborer	3.6
Semiskilled worker	12.5
Skilled worker	4.1
Clerk	5.1
Salesman	8.0
Manager	14.8
Top-level executive	11.6
Owner of small business	16.5
Professional man	16.5
Farm laborer	0.4
Farm owner	5.8
Misc. other	0.1
No answer	0.4

WAS YOUR FATHER A COLLEGE GRADUATE?	%
Yes	26.6
No	73.4
No answer	

IF "YES," DID HE GET ANY ADVANCED DEGREES?	%
Yes	39.3
No	55.4
No answer	5.3

WAS YOUR MOTHER A COLLEGE GRADUATE?	%
Yes	19.6
No	80.3
No answer	0.1

IF "YES," DID SHE GET ANY ADVANCED DEGREES?	%
Yes	10.7
No	72.6
No answer	16.7

Our whole emphasis and interest in the young executives started from our interest in big business. The object of the inquiry was to ascertain something about the young manager who worked for a big company. Of the respondents, 32.7 percent worked for companies whose annual sales came to between $100 and $300 million, 18.9 percent worked for giants whose sales ran over one billion dollars. The particulars:

WHAT IS THE APPROXIMATE SALES VOLUME OF THE COMPANY YOU WORK FOR AT PRESENT?	Total %	TYPE OF BUSINESS Manufacturing %	All Other %
under $50 million	3.9	3.3	4.7
$50-$100 million	4.4	2.8	6.5
$100-$300 million	32.7	37.6	26.5
$300-$500 million	14.6	16.9	11.4
$500 million-$1 billion	17.9	19.1	16.4
over $1 billion	18.9	18.9	18.9
no answer	7.6	1.4	15.9

Their occupations were well scattered:

WHAT TYPE OF BUSINESS OR INDUSTRY ARE YOU IN?	%
MANUFACTURING	
Chemicals, plastics, etc.	6.6
Electronics, electronic equipment, electrical mfg.	10.7
Food, food products	9.3

MANUFACTURING	%
Building materials	1.6
Appliances, home appliances	3.9
Toiletries, pharmaceuticals, drugs	3.3
Textiles, clothing, apparel	4.4
Primary metals	2.8
Machinery (except electrical)	5.7
Misc. other manufacturing and manuf. unspecified	9.1
Insurance	10.2
Transportation	6.7
Banking	9.3
All other financial	1.0
Wholesale, retail	5.9
Public utilities	5.0
Construction	0.6
Communication	0.8
Misc. other business	1.0
Business not specified but product or title given	1.3
No answer	0.8

And they are positioned in the upper ranks of management:

WHAT IS YOUR FULL OFFICIAL TITLE OR POSITION (BRIEF DESCRIPTION OF JOB TITLE)?	%
TOP EXECUTIVES	
President	2.0
Vice-President	19.6
Secretary	2.9
Treasurer	2.3
Comptroller	3.1
General Manager	4.4
All other top executives (chairman of the board, etc.)	1.3
MANAGERS	
Administration, finance, accounting	19.8
Sales, promotion, advert., merch.	17.2

MANAGERS	%
Production, factory	8.6
Chief engineer	4.1
Purchasing agent, buyer	1.5
Laboratory director	0.6
All other managers and unspec. managers	6.6

PROFESSIONAL	
Attorney	3.2
All other professions	1.5
No answer	1.3

In the new business environment, the job that the young manager holds is also fairly new. One third of these men (32.3 percent) are holding jobs that were created when they stepped into them. And of the 67.5 percent who hold jobs which had belonged to other men before them, 20.4 percent had only one predecessor.

ARE YOU THE FIRST MAN TO HOLD THAT JOB?	%
Yes	32.3
No	67.5
No answer	0.2

IF "NO," ABOUT HOW MANY INCUMBENTS WOULD YOU SAY THERE HAVE BEEN?	%
One	20.4
Two	19.0
Three	15.4
Four	8.1
Five	7.5
Six	6.8
Seven	1.8
Eight	0.9
Nine	0.4
Ten or more	6.1
No answer	13.6

And very few of them seem to owe very much to Dad or father-in-law, at least as far as their present position in the company goes: only 1.8 percent said they had relatives who were their superiors in the company.

As a good competitor, the young executive believes in the value of competition—he finds it, as these answers show, "in no way destructive." And he believes, with a really astonishing faith, in the merit system:

WOULD YOU DESCRIBE THE EFFORT TOWARD INSIDE-THE-COMPANY PROMOTIONS IN YOUR COMPANY AS:	%
A real cutthroat struggle	4.2
Highly competitive but in no way destructive	74.7
Not very competitive since it is usually pretty clear to whom the promotion is going	17.1
No answer	4.0

IN YOUR VIEW, DO PROMOTIONS USUALLY GO TO THE MEN WHO REALLY MERIT THEM?	%
Yes	91.0
No	6.3
No answer	2.7

That is why he works so hard:

HOW MANY HOURS A WEEK DO YOU WORK (INCLUDE TIME SPENT IN THE OFFICE AND AWAY FROM THE OFFICE)?	%
Less than 35 hours	0.6
35-39 hours	1.4
40-44 "	8.5
45-49 "	18.3
50-54 "	29.3
55-59 "	17.0
60-64 "	16.2
65 hours or more	7.6
No answer	1.1

How Many Days Do You Travel in a Typical Working Month?	%
1	10.9
2	13.2
3	13.2
4	11.0
5	11.5
6-7	8.5
8-9	5.9
10-14	9.2
15 or more	3.0
None, don't travel	12.1
No answer	1.5

Giving so much to the organization, he gets a good deal in return. When it comes to annual salaries, the range seems to fall between about $20,000 on the low end of the scale and $75,000 at the high end. The difficulty in ascertaining exact salaries came not so much from the reticence of the young executive to talk about what he makes as from the complexity of the kinds of compensation: stock options and a wide range of hard-to-measure company benefits made it impossible to determine exact salary levels.

Among the "fringe" benefits:

Which of the Following Company Benefit Programs Do You Enjoy?	%
A profit sharing plan	44.7
Stock options	49.6
Life insurance	93.2
Health insurance	90.8
Retirement, pension plan, deferred compensation, annuity	32.4
Disability pay	2.1
Travel accident, travel insurance	1.7
Company savings plan, savings, thrift plan	3.0
Bonus plan, bonus incentive program	8.8
Misc. others	3.4
No answer	0.6

IF YOU PARTICIPATE IN A STOCK OPTION
OR PROFIT SHARING PLAN, DO YOU EX-
PECT THAT IT WILL MEAN A SUB-
STANTIAL AMOUNT OF MONEY TO YOU
SOMEDAY?

	%
Yes	73.2
No	19.3
No answer	7.5

WHAT IS THE PRESENT APPROXIMATE
VALUE OF YOUR FAMILY'S LIQUID AS-
SETS?

	%
Less than $2,000	10.1
$2,000-4,999	10.6
$5,000-9,999	13.3
$10,000-14,999	11.7
$15,000-19,999	6.5
$20,000-24,999	6.8
$25,000-29,999	5.6
$30,000-39,999	7.4
$40,000-59,999	6.6
$60,000-99,999	6.0
$100,000-199,999	6.1
$200,000 and over	5.3
No answer	4.0

While average liquid assets were over $49,000, about half
the members of the group were worth less than $20,000.

His political views. The young executive is a Republican.
But there are some interesting gradations here. He is, to begin
with, even more of a Republican than his father was, a reflec-
tion, perhaps, of the somewhat higher social status that he
holds:

ARE YOU REGISTERED IN A POLITICAL
PARTY?

	%
Yes	79.3
No	20.3
No answer	0.4

IF "YES," WHICH ONE?

	%
Republican	80.1
Democratic	19.5

IF "YES," WHICH ONE?	%
Independent	0.3
No answer	0.1

WHAT POLITICAL PARTY DID YOUR FATHER FAVOR?	%
Democratic	36.5
Republican	53.1
Independent, switched, varied	3.1
Conservative	0.3
No answer	7.0

Fortune's formal deadline for answers to this questionnaire was January 31, 1964. Virtually all the replies came in by the middle of February of that year. At that time, Barry Goldwater was the clear spokesman for conservatism in American life, but he had not yet become the inept and confusing figure that he turned out to be following his nomination. When the voting time came, some of the young executives who had found Goldwater a sympathetic figure earlier may have changed their minds. One year later, in January, 1965, a different group of executives (the chairmen or the presidents of 300 of the largest U.S. corporations) was asked by *Fortune:* "In 1960, for whom did you vote? In 1964, for whom did you vote? Principal reason for switching?" Exactly 100 executives replied. Twenty-nine indicated that they had switched to the Democratic candidate in 1964 after having voted for Nixon in 1960. Only 11 percent of the nation's voters as a whole made a similar switch.

OF THE 100 WHO REPLIED:

1. In 1960, for whom did you vote?

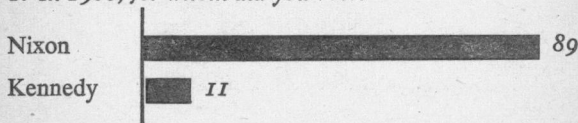

Nixon   89

Kennedy   11

2. In 1964, for whom did you vote?

Goldwater   60

Johnson   40

OF THE 29 WHO SWITCHED

3. *Principal reason for switching?*

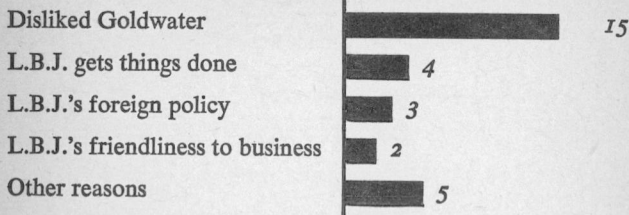

Disliked Goldwater ████████████████████████ *15*

L.B.J. gets things done ████ *4*

L.B.J.'s foreign policy ███ *3*

L.B.J.'s friendliness to business ██ *2*

Other reasons █████ *5*

We do not know, of course, whether a similar switch took place in our group.

But at the point in time when they were replying to our questions, the young executives liked Barry. Four years before, they had liked Nixon even more:

WHAT CANDIDATE, AMONG THE PRESIDENTIAL ASPIRANTS, COMES CLOSEST TO REPRESENTING YOUR VIEWS?	%
Goldwater	24.8
Johnson	23.3
Nixon	14.7
Rockefeller	8.6
Romney	5.2
Lodge	3.1
Scranton	3.9
Eisenhower	0.4
Stevenson	0.4
Misc. others	1.1
None	4.5
No answer	10.0
* (more than one candidate given)	4.4

FOR WHOM DID YOU VOTE IN THE LAST ELECTION?	%
Kennedy	22.3
Nixon	72.8
Not eligible, ill, did not vote	2.3
No answer	2.6

* When more than one candidate was listed the first one listed was taken.

Not without some pleasure, a good many young executives describe themselves as "conservative." And it looks as though many of them are against just as many things as they are for. But perhaps it is just as surprising to note that over 10 percent of these men look on themselves as "liberals."

PLEASE CHARACTERIZE YOUR POLITICAL PHILOSOPHY	%
GENERAL ORIENTATION	
Liberal, progressive, "Bury Goldwater," liberal Democrat, liberal Republican, progressive Republican	10.4
Jeffersonian liberal, moderate liberal, old-fashioned liberal without extremes, middle-of-the-road liberal, liberal toward the center, realistic liberal	4.0
Middle of the road, liberal to conservative, moderate, middle-of-the-road Republican	8.5
Middle-of-the-road conservative, right of center, liberal conservatism	11.7
Conservative, right, well right of center, ultra-conservative, agree with Goldwater	15.5
Independent, practical, vote for man who has my views, Democrat, Republican	7.4
SPECIFIC ISSUES	
For integration, civil rights	6.1
For slow progress in integration, anti-civil rights	0.9
For social welfare, education, health, gov't. help in social welfare	6.7

GENERAL ORIENTATION	%
Against socialism, socialistic programs, Medicare	9.5
Against large, strong, big gov't. (unspecified or political)	19.3
Against government interference in business	8.0

PLEASE CHARACTERIZE YOUR POLITICAL PHILOSOPHY	REGISTERED IN A POLITICAL PARTY		NOT REGISTERED
	Republican %	Democratic %	%
GENERAL ORIENTATION			
Liberal, progressive, "Bury Goldwater," liberal Democrat, liberal Republican, progressive Republican	7.8	20.0	10.8
Jeffersonian liberal, moderate liberal, old-fashioned liberal without extremes, middle-of-the-road liberal, liberal toward the center, realistic liberal	2.2	8.4	5.9
Middle of the road, liberal to conservative, moderate, middle-of-the-road Republican	8.6	5.2	9.8
Middle-of-the-road conservative, right of center, liberal conservatism	13.2	5.2	11.8
Conservative, right, well right of center, ultra-conservative, agree with Goldwater	18.8	9.7	9.3
Independent, practical, vote for man who has my views, Democrat, Republican	4.7	9.7	14.2

SPECIFIC ISSUES	%	%	%
For integration, civil rights	6.1	9.0	3.9
For slow progress in integration, anti-civil rights	0.8	1.3	1.0
For social welfare, education, health, gov't. help in social welfare	6.1	9.0	6.9
Against socialism, socialistic programs, Medicare	10.4	7.1	8.8
Against large, strong, big gov't. (unspecified or political)	21.4	14.8	16.7
Against government interference in business	9.4	7.7	3.9

The extent to which he works for his political views:

DO YOU WORK FOR YOUR POLITICAL PARTY?	%
Yes	25.7
No	72.3
No answer	2.0

IF "YES," AT WHAT LEVEL?	%
Local	91.9
State	16.3
National	8.5
No answer	3.1

IF "YES," WHAT SPECIFICALLY DO YOU DO?	%
Canvassing, campaigning door-to-door, getting out vote	33.3
Elective office: committeeman, county chairman, V.P. of Democratic club, etc.	17.1
Fund raising	20.9
Financial contributor	14.0

IF "YES," WHAT SPECIFICALLY DO YOU DO?	%
Work for candidates, precinct worker, block chairman	28.3
Poll watcher	4.3
Pass out pamphlets, literature	4.7
Miscellaneous	8.9
No answer	5.8

So accustomed to organization in his business life, the young executive seems to be something of a joiner in his leisure time:

TO WHAT CIVIC ORGANIZATIONS DO YOU BELONG? TO WHAT CLUBS DO YOU BELONG?	%
Education, youth (Boy Scouts, Big Brothers, School Board, PTA)	17.9
Religious, church affiliated (Church club, K of C, Holy Name Society, Jewish Federation, YMCA, etc.)	16.1
Country club, Golf club	20.9
Chamber of Commerce, Jr. C. of C., Jaycees	17.0
Political, non-partisan, civic, taxpayers'	14.2
Hobby—except Sports (Bridge club, Coin club, Dance club)	2.7
Social (Luncheon club, Toastmasters, Men's club, Playboy Club)	10.2
Alumni, college (Local college club, etc.)	12.5
Welfare, eleemosynary (Child Service, Rehabilitation Center, Industries for the Blind, Red Cross, USO Council, United Fund)	8.9

To What Civic Organizations Do You Belong? To What Clubs Do You Belong?	%
Business (Manufacturers' Ass'n., Advertising Club, Board of Trade)	10.2
Sports—except golf (Swimming, Beach, Tennis, etc.)	15.6
Fraternal (Elks, Masons, Shrine, etc.)	6.9
Medical, hospital (Cancer Soc., etc.)	2.3
Music, Art, Drama, Literary (Art Institute, Symphony, etc.)	3.6
Professional (Bar Ass'n., Press Club, AMA)	16.4
Service (Kiwanis, Rotary, Lions)	6.2
Boards (appointive, elective) public office (Water Committee, etc.)	2.4
Political—partisan (Republican Club, Reform Democratic Club)	2.3
Veterans, military (Amer. Legion, etc.)	2.1
"Many," "too many"	0.4
Misc.	6.8
None	14.6
No answer	8.2

The ethical question. Views on ethical questions are probably impossible to penetrate with a questionnaire. Talks with individual members of the executive group were far more rewarding than these answers. These do not show any particular preoccupation with ethical matters:

Does the Question of Your Own Ethical Conduct Come Up in Your Business?	%
Very often	8.4
Frequently	18.3
Once in a while	31.4
Almost never	41.4
No answer	0.5

Generally, he seems happy with the ethical condition of the business world:

HAVE YOU ANY GENERAL COMMENT ABOUT THE RELATIONSHIP BETWEEN ETHICAL CONDUCT AND BUSINESS LIFE?	%
Ethical conduct *improves business,* it's necessary to succeed, ethical conduct and business life are *identical,* is *important to business*	29.8
It's *no problem* for business people to keep their noses clean	6.0
Same as in private life, family, community	6.1
Ethics *are high in my business,* my field, no problem in *my* company	5.1
One *cannot compromise* when question arises, I shall resign if I recognize a variance between my business life and ethical conduct	12.4
Ethical standards *are improving,* are better than expected, businessmen are becoming more sensitive to it	1.4
High ethical conduct is *necessary for happiness,* peace of mind	2.7
Necessity of competition, of ever-increasing prices, corporate interests *create unethical conduct,* it may be necessary for survival	4.1
There is unethical conduct, need for improvement, ethical conduct is deteriorating, is nonexistent in business life	7.1
Miscellaneous	6.5
No answer	21.7

At the questionnaire's end, some effort was made to draw out the young executive on his own views about the "organization man" concept. The replies show that he is a rare man who thinks that individual authority has been replaced by the abstraction of the organization; more by far have decided that there is plenty that the individual can do within the organization:

PLEASE INDICATE HOW YOU FEEL ABOUT THIS QUOTATION: "ORGANIZATION REPLACES INDIVIDUAL AUTHORITY; NO INDIVIDUAL IS POWERFUL ENOUGH TO DO MUCH DAMAGE"	%
AGREE	
True—agree (otherwise not specified)	*3.1*
Not powerful enough to do much damage or much good, there is no indispensable man	*3.2*
QUALIFIED	
Not always true, lukewarm, partially true (otherwise not specified)	*5.1*
Depends on the organization, depends on size of company, organizational structure	*4.6*
Basically *true except where a strong individual* heads the organization	*4.1*
DISAGREE	
Incorrect—false (otherwise not specified)	*18.2*
Not true because an *individual can do much damage* and has, e.g. Montgomery Ward; H. Hughes	*19.2*
An individual can still sway an organization if he wants to accomplish his program, decisions are still needed	*24.2*
Organization sets the ground rules only, it channels individual authority, but does not replace it	*20.2*
Nuts, nonsense, ridiculous	*7.8*
Non sequitur, silly quotation	*1.5*
Miscellaneous	*3.2*
No answer	*4.5*

PLEASE INDICATE HOW YOU FEEL ABOUT THIS QUOTATION: "IN A GROUP . . . YOU FEEL A STRONG IMPULSE TO SEEK COMMON GROUND WITH THE OTHERS. THE GROUP IS INSTINCTIVELY HOSTILE TO WHAT IS DIVISIVE. THE URGE IS TO UNITY (AND) IT IS OBSCURING THE FUNCTION OF LEADERSHIP."	%

AGREE

Agree, true (otherwise not specified) — *12.2*

We *all tend to be followers*, it's easier to hide in the crowd, too many "yes" men — *9.7*

This is why *committees cannot run an organization*, uniformity for uniformity's sake is cancerous — *4.8*

QUALIFIED

Partially true; true *but:* the leader must step ahead, with a strong group leader most of the others will be followers — *14.5*

Both unity and individuality are needed, a common ground has to be found — *11.4*

DISAGREE

Disagree—false (otherwise unspecified) — *8.9*

Group *needs a leader*, seeks one, demands one — *8.5*

Strong individuals will make themselves felt, not true of leaders — *16.7*

Not true, *the function of leadership is to encourage ideas*, to evaluate and decide — *8.9*

Not true in my organization, field, stick to my view — *10.7*

Miscellaneous — *3.0*

No answer — *9.7*

PLEASE INDICATE HOW YOU FEEL ABOUT THIS QUOTATION: "THE COMPLEXITY OF MODERN SOCIETY AND THE OMNIPRESENCE OF LARGE-SCALE ORGANIZATIONS ACTUALLY PLACE A PREMIUM ON THE EXERCISE OF A GREATER MEASURE OF RESPONSIBILITY BY MORE PEOPLE THAN EVER BEFORE."	%
AGREE	
Agree, true (otherwise unspecified)	44.8
True, more organizations are putting responsibility on the *lower echelons*	6.8
True, because of *larger organizations, more people,* larger population	11.8
True, because of *more complexity* and more specialization in business today	8.5
True, but often *overdivision* of responsibility and overspecialization are detrimental	1.2
True, but *many do not realize the extent of their responsibility,* the shirker can duck	6.3
Misc. "true" specific reasons	5.2
DISAGREE	
Disagree—no (otherwise unspecified)	1.5
Disagree, because the *few at the top* actually have the responsibility to make the decisions, more and more responsibility in fewer hands	7.0
Misc. unfavorable—specific reasons	1.6
General misc. (perhaps, etc.)	2.0
Poorly stated, should be reworded	4.7
No answer	4.8

Those respondents who replied "No" to the question "Do you think that a high proportion of executives are correctly described by the stereotype of the organization man, as portrayed in currently popular books," went on to explain their disagreement in these terms:

Most executives are individuals and not organization men. Most executives are not just organization men, are outspoken, creative, innovative, have individual methods to exert authority. Not status seeking, pyramid climbing. May be true of a few, but not of most. (Stated in general, *not* with reference to respondent's acquaintances.)   *11.0*

Not those I see, I come in contact with, in *my* experience, in *my* company, in *my* field, in *my* part of the country—they are individualistic, intelligent, better qualified, hardworking, sensitive   *19.9*

Hard-working, not glamorous, not luxury-seeking, sex-maniacs, alcoholics, high-spending, enjoying costly fringe benefits; have well-balanced home lives, are ethical.   *7.8*

Generalizations, exaggerations are not true, depict only a small group, art forms deal with extremes, books overdo it, is pictured the way fiction writers would like to see them; currently popular books written to make money.   *26.6*

There is no "stereotype," was unable to "type" them, the stereotype applies only to superficial characteristics, does not describe a high proportion of executives, they are like other people.   *18.6*

True of middle management, of junior executives, but *not of top management.*   *4.5*

Miscellaneous (If person becomes stereotype it is only a sign of inner weakness. Depends upon individual and circumstances. They are not truly executives and will sooner or later destroy themselves or their company.)   *8.9*

A geographic breakdown was arrived at by the postmarks on the envelopes:

DISTRIBUTION BY STATE (FROM POSTMARK)	%
NEW ENGLAND	
Maine	
New Hampshire	
Vermont	
Massachusetts	
Rhode Island	
Connecticut	
Total New England	6.6
MIDDLE ATLANTIC	
New York	
New Jersey	
Pennsylvania	
Total Middle Atlantic	35.4
EAST NORTH CENTRAL	
Ohio	
Indiana	
Illinois	
Michigan	
Wisconsin	
Total East North Central	24.3
WEST NORTH CENTRAL	
Minnesota	
Iowa	
Missouri	
North Dakota	
South Dakota	
Nebraska	
Kansas	
Total West North Central	6.6
SOUTH ATLANTIC	
Delaware	
Maryland	
District of Columbia	
Virginia	
West Virginia	

SOUTH ATLANTIC %
North Carolina
South Carolina
Georgia
Florida
    Total South Atlantic 5.9

EAST SOUTH CENTRAL
Kentucky
Tennessee
Alabama
Mississippi
    Total East South Central 2.0

WEST SOUTH CENTRAL
Arkansas
Louisiana
Oklahoma
Texas
    Total West South Central 5.0

MOUNTAIN
Montana
Idaho
Wyoming
Colorado
New Mexico
Arizona
Utah
Nevada
    Total Mountain 1.0

PACIFIC
Washington
Oregon
California
Alaska
Hawaii
    Total Pacific 11.9

State unknown 1.0

Outside U.S. 0.3

Chapter ELEVEN

Toward the Journey's End

With his natural bent for assessment, the young executive often scrutinizes his own future prospects. But it is characteristic of him that he does not try to see beyond the next couple of rungs on the corporate ladder. His immediate objectives usually engage all of his attention, not only in terms of the business problem he confronts, but also in terms of his own place in the hierarchy: he may envision himself doing the job of an immediate superior, but he rarely wants to look much beyond that—too much can intervene, he thinks, and why should he waste his time and his emotional energy?

In rare moments of introspection, however, he does ponder the question, as he phrases it, "of going all the way." Feelings in those moments are ambivalent, and their true meaning is hard to plumb. In general, it is clear that this point—"going all the way"—touches one of the young manager's most sensitive nerves. He does not often say exactly what he means in response to it. It may be one of the few areas where, because of his attentive eye on the possibility of corporate embarrassment, he is less than frank. But it is hard to avoid the judgment that it means a great deal to him, and that he will suffer some fiery ordeals if he doesn't make it to the top.

A few men in this group frankly declare that their goal is to be president of the company. They will be content with nothing less. One man who now reports to one of his company's executive vice-presidents, and who knows that an executive vice-presidency will be opening up soon, was asked if he wants the job. He replied: "No. I want to be president." Another man not yet forty who works for a billion-dollar insurance company says, "To be president of this company is my objective." But he adds: "When I'm ready, the company may not be ready for me. Its needs may be for another type."

The added caution is pertinent. Knowing corporate life as he does, this man is aware that the selection of a chief executive depends on many factors. The needs of the industry as a whole, the condition of the company at the time, the strengths of the men who will surround the new chief executive, all must be taken into account. Some men who in other times might be chosen as chief executives will be passed over because, at that moment in history, the company needs talents different from theirs.

Right now the young executive thinks he will be able to accept that judgment of the system without complaint or bitterness. "I wouldn't feel unhappy," asserts one. "I can still compete in other ways. I wouldn't feel a failure if I didn't make it." Agrees another: "My reaction is to take it as it comes. I see a lot of people in this company around my age whom I feel great respect for; they're as good as I am. If I make it, fine. If I don't, that's all right too."

Another man tries to spell out his responses in this way: "Look, I feel I owe this company something. If I didn't, I wouldn't be here. So long as I'm fairly treated, I don't mean spoiled, I feel an obligation to continue to give what I've got, to stay with it. It's not a binding obligation but it's some obligation. If they keep being good to me, I haven't any reason to complain. I don't have any special aspirations as to what I'm called or where I rank as long as I can accomplish something that to me is interesting, mentally challenging work. I want to be fairly compensated. If I can give my children the things I want to give them—and that has limitations to it, I don't want to leave each of them a million, but I've got five and I want to leave each about $100,000, and I think I can do it—I really haven't any other ambition. Today I make around $35,000. And that's going to get better before long.

"I won't feel a failure if I don't make the board of directors. I'd be happy as a district supervisor somewhere, where I would have time to coach the basketball team. As far as the board goes—I don't think I'll ever be as frustrated as some of the people already there. That kind of ambition can be unhealthy. And nobody in my family gives a hoot in hell."

Another man puts his own reactions in the framework he uses to weigh the people who work for him: "With the people under me," he says, "I avoid trying to pick the ones who may be board members someday. I think I can see whether they'll get to my level, or my boss's. Who gets to the top depends on circumstances—a fellow gets into a spot, and has an opportunity. I think I'll progress beyond my present point. If someone got a job I wanted, I might be upset, but that hasn't happened yet."

Yet one senses that such responses are somehow out of character. The man is so constructed that he believes in changes he can effect, and in the personal role he plays in controlling his own destiny. He has never during his business career taken a passive attitude toward "circumstances," and he had never really had a very high opinion of people who do—in his view, they are attributing to "circumstances" failures which are better explained by inadequacies within themselves. Circumstances serve them as camouflage.

The young executive often says that luck has played a role in his successes. "I've come so far from that dirty little town I was born in," one man remarks, and an ingenuous kind of wonder sounds in his voice. But the young executive also agrees with Emerson that "luck favors the prepared mind"; it comes most readily, he thinks, to those who have worked for it, are ready to receive it, and are quick to recognize it and capitalize on it.

One man who works for the giant U. S. Steel Corporation, and who has outstripped all the men of his age in his department sums up the reasons for his frequent promotions this way: "Good fortune has a lot to do with it. But that is only one element. I think mental attitude has a great deal of importance. Many fellows I've worked with have been much smarter than I am, but temperamental, and when the going got tough they just didn't handle it. Some broke up under pressure. Some, with no pressure, broke down and just didn't do anything. Mental conditioning was part of my education. Then one of the important things is desire—I wanted it." Again sounds the old refrain: work and you win.

So when the young executive sounds cheerful about how he would react if he lost the big one, he may be whistling in the dark. Some of these men, by the time they come to the point where they can no longer move ahead, may have enough acres of responsibility to plow, and they may be content. But many of them may not be. The young executive often remarks generously of contemporaries whom he has left behind that "they're good solid men, they make their contribution"—but that valedictory, easy enough for him to call back over his shoulder for someone else, is far too patronizing to suffice for himself. He hopes for a grander and more eloquent epitaph than that, which belongs on the headstone of lesser mortals—the people he has left to carry on the important, but lesser, function of bringing up the rear. He wants to make it to the pinnacle. If the band doesn't play when his climb ends, he is in for some poignant moments—and, while obviously there is no evidence to cite in support of the point, one might expect his whole strong, ego-centered psychological house to be shaken severely then. How he will manage will be a fascinating study for some journalist in the future.

Inner resources are hard to weigh. There are no certainties for any man. But it is worth considering, by way of prediction, that neither the money he has worked for nor the pleasures of contemplative thought that others can experience will have the power to solace the young executive very much. His personal needs will have diminished, and money will have sunk even from its present secondary status as a motivating force. And some of his intellectual muscles, the ones that some men have soared on, may have withered away. The trenchancy of work will be gone. He will have to look for a new context for his life—a hard job for someone long unaware that any other context existed.

Perhaps he will not be helped, either, by the fact that only a few people in his company, and a few professional colleagues outside of it, know of his triumphs. In the view of society at large, the young executive's role has always been anonymous: he is, to society, one of the nameless tinkerers whose small adjustments remain forever invisible or indistinguishable from a thousand others which may add up to a great result, but which bear no personal cachet. Right now, the young executive accepts—or says he accepts—his anonymity with total unconcern. "Fame? Who needs it?" The young man shrugs. "I wouldn't know what to do with it." Another adds: "What I do is going to go unrecognized by the great American public. But who cares? It's recognition inside the company that's important." Still another one, who deplores the attitudes of that "great American public," puts it this way: "I'm convinced what we do just isn't news. Our business is vitally inportant to the community we work in, but I'm sure the community just doesn't understand it, even though we've given plenty of publicity to the point. People feel they have no control over the destiny of the businessman, so they're just not interested. It takes a bigger man than me to believe that you have to have some impact on society."

As with the expression of views on getting to the top, however, these opinions may conceal truer inner feelings. Again, one can only speculate. A poll taken of selected business managers of all ranks and ages not long ago showed that 82 percent of them expressed a willingness to participate in government and political affairs if given an opportunity to do so. Interestingly, the poll showed that the degree of interest went up with the length of service: with men who had spent thirty years or more in business, fully 90 percent wanted to or were willing to take a fling in government or politics. That may permit the hazard that the anonymity of it all chafes a bit after a time. But no one knows now what the young executive's beliefs on that question of fame will be later in life.

But all that seems a long way off. For this realistic young businessman, today is sufficient. He asks only that it challenge his intelligence, test his powers, and demand his best efforts. One division manager for General Electric, who deals with both governmental and private customers, sums up the attitudes of his generation very well. Although he constantly associates with two behemoths—his own company and the U. S. Government—he never feels crushed between the two. His job leaves him plenty of latitude and gives him plenty of stimulus. "The important challenge is in the job," he says. "It isn't a matter of earning more money. A more interesting question is whether I would take less money to keep working in aerospace, where the challenge lies for me. I see some tough days ahead, with the Defense Department's budget cut and consequent confusion in some of our customer areas. If those days come, I'd take less money to keep doing this job."

As long as business problems throw down the challenge—and the overworked word exactly reflects the young man's view of it—the young executive will take it up and be aroused by it. He asks only that they increase in scope and complexity as his experience increases—a progression that seems sure to take place. When that happens, he will respond with his own independent judgments, never looking for safety in a mold.

Perhaps the most fundamental reason for that comes not from company policy, or even from the character of the man himself. It arises out of the very nature of the situations that the man must cope with. Each of those situations is met only once. None will occur again in quite the same form, or remain tomorrow what it was yesterday. The uniqueness of the situations makes it impossible to discover what kind of action within their framework would constitute conformity. Even if he would, the young executive could not find an archetype for his behavior in these complicated and fluid circumstances. There is no archetype.

His authority of course has its limits. But every man, everywhere, has known such limits. The ones that these men were bounded by chafed no more than the ones that most people sustain in their lifetimes. Within the limits, the young executive finds plenty of room for freedom of action. He always wants more. But he has already found a good deal.

Appendix

The Questionnaire

CONFIDENTIAL QUESTIONNAIRE

FORTUNE Magazine is engaged in collecting information about the younger man in American business, preparatory to a FORTUNE series about that man.

In order to obtain a rounded portrait, we need a good deal of what might be considered personal information. We want to assure you, however, that the information requested in the questionnaire below will be treated as confidential—in fact, it cannot be traced back to you or to your company.

We are most grateful for your help.

A FEW BASIC FACTS ABOUT YOU AND YOUR FAMILY . . .

1. Your year of birth:_____

2. Are you: single......☐
          widowed ...☐
          divorced ...☐.......(how many times?_____)
          married....☐.......(how many times?_____)

3. a) How many children do you have?
    _____boy(s)   _____girl(s)

b) Are any of your children attending
private school   Yes...☐   No...☐
private college   Yes...☐   No...☐

4. Is your wife a college graduate?   Yes...☐   No...☐

5. a) What was the *highest* level you attained in school?
grade school........................☐
attended high school ....☐
graduated high school ....☐
attended college ....☐
graduated college ....☐
post-graduate ....☐

b) If you went to college, was it
an Ivy League school ....☐
a private school (other than Ivy League)......☐
a state university or college ....☐
a city university or college ....☐

c) If you graduated from college, in what field of study did you get your undergraduate degree?

d) Academic honors, if any:_____

e) What graduate degree(s), if any, did you get?_____

_____

f) Did you attend night school?   Yes...☐   No...☐
If "yes," what degree(s) did you get as a direct result of night school courses?

6. a) Did you contribute to the cost of your education by outside work?

Yes...☐   No...☐

b) If "yes," how much?
a small amount ....☐
about half the cost........☐
more than half...........☐

c) Did you hold any scholarship(s)?

Yes...☐   No...☐

7. a) If you could start your formal schooling over again, would you choose the same field of study?

Yes...☐   No...☐

b) If "no," what field would you choose?_____

_____

Please state briefly why:_____

_____

_____

_____

8. a) Where did you grow up?
   in a big metropolitan center or its suburbs.....□
   in a city of 100,000 to
         500,000 population.....□
   in a city of 50,000 to
         100,000 population......□
   in a small town or rural area.................□

   b) In what state(s) did you spend the first ten years of your life?

   _____

ABOUT YOUR LIFE TODAY . . .

I. a) What type of dwelling do you live in?
     apartment ....□
     single-family house ....□
     other ....□

   b) If you own your own house, what is its estimated market value today?
             $_____

   c) When was your house built?
        Year:_____

2. a) How many cars do you and your *immediate* family now own? _____
           (number)

   b) Please list:

Make(s) now owned	Year of model	Bought New	Used
_____ .. _____		□	□
_____ .. _____		□	□
_____ .. _____		□	□

3. Do you belong to a country club? Yes....□ No....□

4. What are your hobbies?_____
   _____
   _____

5. What sports do you regularly enjoy?
   as a spectator: _____
   _____

   as a participant: _____
   _____

6. Please list the magazines of all kinds which you read regularly:
   _____
   _____
   _____
   _____

7. a) About how many books, *unrelated* to your business, have you read in the past year?_____

   b) If you can recall any of the titles, please list a few:
   _____
   _____
   _____

8. a) About how many books, *related* to your business, have you read in the past year?_____

   b) If you can recall any of the titles, please list a few:____
   _____
   _____
   _____

9. Is there a difference between the reading you do in your office and the reading you do at home?
   Yes, I read completely different material...........☐
   No, my home reading is usually directly or indirectly
   related to my office work.......................☐

ABOUT YOUR WORK . . .

1. At what level did you begin your business career?
   laborer ....☐
   semiskilled worker ....☐
   skilled worker ....☐
   lower ranks of management ....☐
   middle ranks of management ....☐

at the top ....□
other (please specify) _____

2. Where do you work at the present time? (Please check the appropriate box(es):

I work in the same town where I was brought up.....□
I work in the same state where I was brought up.....□
I work within 100 miles of the place where I was
brought up ....□
I work over 100 miles from the place where I
was brought up ....□

3. What is the approximate sales volume of the company you work for at present?

under $50 million...................□
$50-$100 million ....□
$100-$300 million ....□
$300-$500 million ....□
$500-$1 billion ....□
over $1 billion ....□

4. a) What type of business or industry are you in?_____
   _____

   b) Major product or service of your company:_____
   _____

5. What is your full official title or position (brief description of job title)?
   _____
   _____

6. Are you the first man to hold that job?
   Yes....□   No....□
   If "no," about how many incumbents would you say there have been?_____

7. Do you have relatives who are your superiors in your present company?
   Yes....□   No....□

8. How long have you been with your present company?
   _____years

9. a) Have you worked for companies other than your present company?
   Yes....□   No....□
   If "yes," a) for how many years in total?_____

         b) how many times have you moved from one company to another in your adult business life?_____

10. Which of the following considerations were most important to you when you made a move: (You may check more than one)

I was blocked on my old job, and saw an opportunity to move ahead faster somewhere else ....☐

I moved because I got more money immediately, as well as a more promising future..........☐

My old situation was pretty intolerable, and I wanted a change.............................☐

I felt I had a couple of strikes against me on my record in my old job, and I wanted a fresh start ....☐

11. What is the greatest single source of satisfaction to you on your present job?

The sense of accomplishment I get from it........☐

The fact that it pays very well...................☐

The belief that if I perform well, I've got a good future here...............................☐

I have some real creative opportunities right now, as well as promise for the future..............☐

The knowledge that if I perform ably, I am secure in my tenure, and should have a decent retirement ....☐

12. What is the greatest source of dissatisfaction?

The company is too big, and I never get a real sense of accomplishment as a result of my own performance ....☐

I don't make enough money to get myself and my family the things we want...................☐

Uniformity is imposed, and I never really get a chance to express my individual, dissenting beliefs ....☐

The company thinks the group or committee have to be harmonious around here, and I secretly hate harmony ....☐

13. Would you describe the effort toward inside-the-company promotions in your company as:

a real cut-throat struggle.......................☐
highly competitive but in no way destructive.......☐
not very competitive since it is usually pretty
clear to whom the promotion is going............☐

14. In your view, do promotions usually go to the men who really merit them?

Yes....☐   No....☐

15. How many hours a week do you work (include time spent in the office and away from the office) ?_____

16. Please check among the following statements those which most closely apply in your case:
I work hard, but I make sure I have time left
over for my family, even though it may slow
my business career............................☐
I work hard, but I make sure I have time left
over for my family. I don't think that holds
me back any in my business....................☐
I work so hard that I don't have enough time
for my family right now. But I expect I will
have in a couple of years or so..................☐

17. My wife thinks I spend too much time working.

Yes....☐   No....☐

18. Please check among the following statements those which you feel apply in your case:
My wife has been a very important factor in
my business career............................☐
My wife has been helpful, but not very im-
portant ....☐
My wife's role in my business career has been
negligible, I'm sorry to say.....................☐
My wife's role in my business career has been
negligible, and I'm glad of it...................☐
She had slowed my progress.....................☐

19. How many days do you travel in a typical working month?
_____days

20. a) Which of the following company benefit programs do
you enjoy?
a profit sharing plan.............☐
stock options ....☐

life insurance ....□
health insurance..............□
other (please specify)_____
_____

b) If you participate in a stock option or profit sharing plan, do you expect that it will mean a substantial amount of money to you some day?

Yes....□ No....□

21. What is the present approximate value of your family's liquid assets? (Include cash, checking accounts, all types of savings accounts, corporate stocks and bonds, and government bonds) $_____

ABOUT YOUR PARENTS . . .

1. Was your father . . .
   a laborer..................□
   semiskilled worker.........□
   skilled worker............□
   clerk ....□
   salesman ....□
   manager ....□
   top-level executive.........□
   owner of small business.....□
   professional man ....□
   farm laborer ....□
   farm owner ....□
   other (please specify)_____

2. a) Was your father a college graduate?

Yes....□ No....□

   b) If "yes," did he get any advanced degrees?

Yes....□ No....□

3. a) Was your mother a college graduate?

Yes....□ No....□

   b) If "yes," did she get any advanced degrees?

Yes....□ No....□

4. a) Are both your parents still alive?

Yes....□ No....□

   b) If "no," please check which one has passed away:
                     father...□ mother...□
   c) If father has passed away, how old were you when he died?_____years old

5. How many times did your father move during your childhood?

not at all ....☐
less than five times ....☐
five to ten times ....☐
a great many times ....☐

6. How many children did your parents have?_____

ABOUT YOUR POLITICAL VIEWS . . .

1. a) Are you registered in a political party?

Yes....☐   No....☐

  b) If "yes," which one: Republican........☐
                          Democratic ......☐
                          Other (please specify)_____

  _____

2. What candidate, among the presidential aspirants, comes closest to representing your views?

_____

3. For whom did you vote in the last election?

_____

4. What political party did your father favor?

_____

5. Please characterize your political philosophy:

_____
_____
_____
_____
_____

6. Do you work for your political party?

Yes....☐   No....☐

  If "yes," a) at what level?
              Local ....☐
              State ....☐
              National ....☐

          b) what specifically do you do?

  _____
  _____
  _____

7. To what civic organizations do you belong? (Please list)

_____

_____

_____

_____

8. To what clubs do you belong?

_____

_____

_____

TO CONCLUDE . . .

1. Does the question of your own ethical conduct come up in your business:
   very often ....☐
   frequently ....☐
   once in a while ....☐
   almost never ....☐

2. Have you any general comment about the relationship be-tween ethical conduct and business life?

_____

3. a) Given the fact that more computers seem to be on the way, do you think that:
      This will lessen the responsibility of the in-dividual manager? ....☐
      This will neither increase nor decrease those responsibilities? ....☐
      This will mean that the individual manager has greater responsibility than before? ....☐

   b) Any other comments you care to add?_____

   _____

4. Please indicate how you feel about these quotations:
   "Organization replaces individual authority; no indi-vidual is powerful enough to do much damage."

   _____

   _____

   "In a group . . . you feel a strong impulse to seek com-mon ground with the others. The group is instinctively

hostile to what is divisive. The urge is to unity (and) it is obscuring the function of leadership."

"The complexity of modern society and the omnipresence of large-scale organizations actually place a premium on the exercise of a greater measure of responsibility by more people than ever before."

---

5. a) Do you think that a high proportion of executives are correctly described by the stereotype of the organization man, as portrayed in currently popular books?

Yes....☐   No....☐

b) If "no," please explain:_____

_____

Thank you very much for your help.

Selected Bibliography

Argyris, Chris, *Personality and Organization*. New York: Harper & Brothers, 1957.

Berle, Adolph, *Power without Property*. New York: Harcourt, Brace & Company, 1959.

Boulding, Kenneth, *The Organizational Revolution*. New York: Harper & Brothers, 1953.

Bowen, Howard, *Social Responsibilities of the Businessman*. New York: Harper & Brothers, 1953.

Chase, Stuart, *The Proper Study of Mankind*. New York: Harper & Brothers, 1948.

Dalton, Melville, *Men Who Manage*. New York: John Wiley and Son, 1959.

Dill, Hilton, and Reitman, *The New Managers*. Englewood Cliffs, N.J.: Prentice-Hall, Inc., 1962.

Drucker, Peter, *America's Next Twenty Years*. New York: Harper & Brothers, 1955.

———, *Concept of the Corporation*. Boston: Beacon Press, Inc., 1960. Revised edition, New York: The New American Library, 1964.

———, *The Practice of Management*. New York: Harper & Brothers, 1954.

Falk, Roger, *The Business of Management*. London: Pelican Books, 1961.

Foster, George, *Traditional Cultures and the Impact of Technological Change*. New York: Harper & Row, Inc., 1962.

Frankel, Charles, *The Case for Modern Man*. Boston: Beacon Press, Inc., 1956.

Fromm, Erich, *The Sane Society*. New York: Rinehart & Company, Inc., 1955.

Gardner, John, *Excellence*. New York: Harper & Row, 1961.

———, *Self Renewal, The Individual and Innovative Society*. New York: Harper & Row, 1963.

Griswold, A. Whitney, *Liberal Education and the Democratic Ideal*. New Haven: Yale University Press, 1959.

Hacker, Andrew, "The Elected and the Anointed." *Political Science Review*, September, 1961.

Hand, Learned, *Spirit of Liberty*. New York: Alfred A. Knopf, Inc., 1952.

Harbison, F. H., and Myers, C. A., *Management in the Industrial World*. New York: McGraw-Hill Book Co., 1959.

Hook, Sidney, *The Paradoxes of Freedom*. Berkeley: University of California Press, 1962.

————, *Political Power and Personal Freedom*. New York: Criterion Books, Inc., 1959.

Lerner, Max, *America as a Civilization*, 2 vols. New York: Simon & Schuster, Inc., 1957.

McGuire, Joseph, *Business and Society*. New York: McGraw-Hill Book Co., 1963.

Newcomer, Mabel, *The Big Business Executive*. New York: Columbia University Press, 1955.

Reagan, Michael, *The Managed Economy*. New York: Oxford University Press, 1963.

Riesman, David, *Individualism Reconsidered*. Chicago: Free Press, 1955.

————, *The Lonely Crowd*. New Haven: Yale University Press, 1950.

Sayles, Leonard, *Individualism and Big Business*. New York: McGraw-Hill Book Co., 1963.

Walker, Edward, and Heyns, Roger, *An Anatomy for Conformity*. Englewood Cliffs, N. J.: Prentice-Hall, Inc., 1962.

Warner, Lloyd, *American Life: Dream and Reality*. Chicago: University of Chicago Press, 1953.

————, and Martin, Norman, eds., *Industrial Man: Businessmen and Business Organizations*. New York: Harper & Brothers, 1959.

————, and Abegglen, James, *Occupational Mobility*. Minneapolis: University of Minnesota Press, 1955.

Whyte, William H., Jr., *The Organization Man*. New York: Simon & Schuster, Inc., 1956.

Other MENTOR Books You'll Want to Read

THE FUTURE OF INDUSTRIAL MAN
by Peter F. Drucker

This classic study, written during World War II, points out the steps to be taken if our society is to operate freely on an industrial basis. New Introduction by Edward T. Chase.

(#MT625—75¢)

AUTOMATION: Its Impact on Business and People
by Walter Buckingham

The economic and human problems posed by widespread industrial automation are analyzed by an expert.

(#MP525—60¢)

THE FOLKLORE OF MANAGEMENT
by Clarence Randall

A provocative study of modern business methods and of the misconceptions which threaten good management.

(#MP443—60¢)

MEN, WAGES, AND EMPLOYMENT IN THE MODERN U.S. ECONOMY *by George Soule*

A noted economist analyzes present trends in wages, employment, labor, and management. (#MD115—50¢)

TOWARD THE LIBERALLY EDUCATED EXECUTIVE
edited by R. A. Goldwin and C. A. Nelson

Top men in the fields of industry and education analyze the type of leadership needed in business. (#MT669—75¢)

THE THEORY OF BUSINESS ENTERPRISE
by Thorstein Veblen

A stimulating analysis of the development of the industrial system and of the influence of business principles and practice on the basic aspects of our civilization.

(#MP540—60¢)

THE AGE OF AUTOMATION *by Sir Leon Bagrit*

Automation discussed in terms of its liberating effects on man's social and cultural development. By a distinguished British industrialist. (#MP626—60¢)